THE CRUCIBLE OF HUMANITY

A full account of the exchange
between the Sphinx and Oedipus

First published in 2022 by OrtonRoad Books.

16 Salisbury Gardens, Newcastle upon Tyne, NE2 1HP, UK.

ISBN 978-1-9993086-5-0

Self-made gods with only the laws of physics to keep us company we are accountable to no one. We are consequently wreaking havoc on our fellow animals and on the surrounding eco-system, seeking little more than our own comfort and amusement, yet never finding satisfaction.

Is there anything more dangerous than dissatisfied and irresponsible gods who don't know what they want?' Yuval Noah Harari, Sapiens: *A Brief History of Mankind.*

'Man is a useless passion.' Jean-Paul Sartre, *Being and Nothingness.*

'Truth to tell, we do not know who we are - and that is who we are.' John Caputo, *Truth: The Search for Wisdom in the Postmodern Age.*

'How can man know himself? He is a thing dark and veiled; and if the hare has seven skins, man can slough off seventy times seven and still not be able to say: "This is really you, this is no longer outer shell."' Friedrich Nietzsche, *Timely Meditations*

4

Contents

PREFACE

The Saturday Group discussed the riddle of the human for many weeks between early 2020 and mid-2022. The group generated a flow of ideas and a process that became the seed corn of this book. My warmest salutations to fellow group members Leigh Rooney, Tony Ward, Joel Yoeli, Jenny Thomas, Mike Boggon, Anna Regan, Clare Moody, Lucian Peterca, Nigel Collins, Penny Tasker and Mary Whitby for creating a process capable of challenging the social and intellectual norms of engagement. I am indebted to George Dimitri for sharing with me his knowledge of early Greek thought. Andrew Sturgess made the route to publication an easy one.

Roy Sturgess, August 2022.

A: I dreamt I was a butterfly, said Chuang Tzu.

B: I dreamt I was a human, said I.

A: I dreamt the world was my oyster, said Falstaff.

B: We do the best we can anyway, whatever it is.

A: I wish I were more human, say we all.

B: I wish I were a butterfly, said Borges.

Joseph Agassi, *A Philosopher's Apprentice.*

INTRODUCTION

In his play *Oedipus the King* Sophocles put words into the mouth of the Sphinx that echo down the ages. The Sphinx approached humankind as a riddle. And we are forced to concur with her that no theory serves to anchor humans in reality. It is not enough just to say we breathe, eat, work and love. Indeed in postmodern times humans focus attention on themselves to the exclusion of almost everything else and yet an air of dissatisfaction won't go away. Our complexity is our glory; the fluidity of our minds is capable of taking us anywhere – and yet we are estranged from ourselves. We are capable of sublime nobility and forbidding brutality. What can we make of this? Are humans ever to understood themselves? As the early Greeks were wont to ask: Does human complexity preclude the possibility of living an easeful life together? Thankfully philosophy has been around for 2,500 years. It has watched as visions of human potential have grown and vanished; it has observed the awkwardness with which the gift of consciousness has been handled. It offers itself as a method that addresses human estrangement from reality. It is what this book is about.

The Sphinx asks strangers entering Thebes: What is it that walks on four, two and then three legs over a span of time? The answer is: a human. But the crucial point is not the mundane answer demanded by the Sphinx. It is that she challenges the notion of a fixed human condition when she turned the issue into a riddle. She is saying that we can't pin down the complexity of humans to a few

9

salient features. That the myth presents man as the solution to such a dilemma, Roberto Calasso observes, 'suggests the enigmatic nature of man.' (1) It follows that the enigmatic human is incapable of being able to 'know thyself' (a maxim inscribed on the pediment of the temple of Apollo at Delphi). We do not know how to know what a human is, or even if there is anything to know. We cannot explain things away simply as our emergence from the primordial mists or from our own parents. The most we have at the outset is Socrates' acknowledgement that we know we don't know. To go further is impossible. Our ability to reflect back on our thoughts makes us a unique species. But this means there is no measure that helps us understand the possibilities open to us. Indeed the idea of a measure is too rigid to encompass human complexity. We fall back on the measurement of individual faculties such as IQ. But measurement of an isolated faculty doesn't tell us what a human is, in and of itself. We fail when we try to answer the question from a human perspective: a human contemplation of humanity. The Greeks told us we must step outside the human realm altogether and open the mind to concepts like infinity, truth, reality or God if we are to find a context that can embrace all. But a move beyond what is usually meant by humanity suggests we have failed in some crucial way. It suggests we need rescuing from ourselves. This is a possibility humans are loath to address.

A starting point is the metaphor of Oedipus. The people of Thebes suffered from a strange malady after Oedipus became king. Death and distress were everywhere. The city needed cleansing of the stain of an unspecified crime. So we have a benchmark for our questioning of humanity: the intensity and scale of the despair that humans suffer. But, King Oedipus could not put things right, even though he was the very model of a caring, intelligent and involved ruler. Sophocles was telling us that, as much as we may form treaties to stop wars and spend money to relieve poverty, war and poverty remain. Taking action against the symptoms of deep issues is not enough. The Theban malady reflected a deep malaise in human affairs. The symptoms sat above something more deep-rooted, intangible and ungraspable. The fullest explanation - today it might be the mapping of the brain - will never take us there. The arrival of consciousness raises a question over the validity of human perceptions. It challenges claims to experience, logic and theories of everything. Consciousness has turned life into a concept.

The problem is that humans can easily be the opposite of what they set out to be or say they are. We happily say we are a body plus consciousness and yet we can easily imagine ourselves without a body. We have a body, but our experiences float in the air. We have a mind, but hesitate to let it roam where it will. We are not sure we ourselves are real, but we take everything else around us to be so. And so we settle on the broadest of issues, like extinction and survival, and stave off desperation by making our minds, in Hilaire Belloc's words, 'keep a-hold of nurse For fear of finding something worse.' This timidity leads to relativist thinking: everything boils down to a little bit more of this or a little bit less of that. Absolute ideas are cast aside. This is the stance of postmodernism. Yet classical philosophy told us that the human will never be at ease with themselves and the world unless our thinking is free to address the grandest of concepts like reality, truth, infinity or God. Moreover, they suggested that only a mind emptied of all suppositions and particularities can think in this way. A mind thus emptied is free to conceive of wholeness, that is to say, reality. This is our anchorage. These ancient Greek insights inspired the preparation of this book.

God threw down a gauntlet in Genesis when He gave a mind to some animals. We humans lost the immediacy of connection to an animal nature and gained nothing that defines us in return. People might claim they know something, that a sense of purpose or meaning emerges when they explore ideas such as the self, society and being. But these ideas offer us less than the total picture; they tend to be contained within the logic of propositions or causation. We are hit with a double whammy (when we can admit it) because we know we don't know and we don't know what to do with this knowledge. We are in a state of limbo. No wonder some claim that ignorance is bliss.

On the very biggest issues people say: I can't even guess. Heidegger admits we don't know the world or reality. The Israeli thinker Yeshayahu Leibowitz says that people don't even want to know at all. Even more disconcerting, the

Sphinx was telling us we don't know that there's nothing to know. And we can't get to this point of clarity because we are not even living a life authentic enough to act as a basis for gaining knowledge. Sartre says life itself creates human essence and that humans lack the courage to face life. But Sophocles was pointing out that, once we start living, fully living, and only then, reality will sweep away all our worries about particularities; about this, that, or the other. Look for example at Oedipus's own situation: blinded, broken, exiled, and yet reconciled to things. Now we will be able to contemplate the magnificence of the world. Only now will we have lost our fear of entering frank and revealing conversations without first being given a safe remit or agenda. Only in a state of wonderment will we stop taking sides against other people and take the first courageous steps towards reconciliation with ourselves, others and the world.

Human will has replaced nature. We roam the Earth at its expense because we connect to each other and not to the Earth. We believe we bestow meaning on the world but the world already understands truth. We retreat into ourselves when faced with the enormity of life because we treat our fellow humans as a threat to our equanimity. The human was born, but we treat the mind (which distinguishes humankind from other creatures) as a cross to bear. It is difficult not to agree with Nietzsche that human existence floats on a tide of *ressentiment*. Conversations that progress beyond social niceties settle on the ailments or frailty of one or other party or become mutually-reinforcing exchanges of dogmatic opinion. The search for the human settles uneasily on family dispositions, ethnic or identity divisions, administrative roles, social networks, and emotionally-heightened phenomena like social acclaim, celebrity or erotic adventures. But the intimacy with others that everyone craves never materialises. Heidegger's idea of Dasein means 'being there together.' But the coming together of humans can produce feelings of such intensity that they destroy our attempts to be intimate. And so people pull back, vowing never to try again. People are perpetually on the rebound from engagement. Socrates most probably thought this about the people he met in the market place. Literature abounds with such situations.

We search into this aspect or that and never the whole, because there seems to be no method that deals with wholeness. Marx places humanity's essence in society. Heidegger places it in being. Sartre places it in existence. In one corner of a life sits truth, in the other three are reality, society, and self. We juggle their relationship in an attempt to create an optimal life. But things never seem to align. Humans travel to space, transplant human organs, open up brain functions and discover AI, DNA and biotech, and yet we are unable to do anything about war, madness or distress. It seems fair to deduce that the human is a project that has never properly got off the ground, an example of evolutionary arrest.

When we seek certainty we invariably appeal to personal experience. But this move generally ends in tears. Appeals to our own feelings may gain unquestioning approval from those around us, but experience is such a small part of reality. The light it casts pales when compared to the wealth of reality waiting to be explored beyond our own horizons. Great books, the wisdom of the ages, other people, and imagination and conceptualisation tell us so much more. This is why, in the end, questions about the human fall into the lap of philosophy. The pivoting of our thoughts away from the self to the world is the philosopher's stone of classical thinkers. We may think only about ourselves as a first move. But then we can think about 'them' and a lightness settles. Ironically, the mind handles the most sensitive personal things best when it is not concentrating on 'poor me.'

Society's attempt to make humans the measure of all things is a siren call. It appeals only because we humans have lost a sense of our place in the great scheme of things. We have no trust in reality because we don't trust our thinking to clear a way to it. Our failure to stay open to all possibilities means we can't appreciate that the world and our place in it are already perfect. It seems impossible to accept that, beyond attending to our basic daily needs, we need do nothing. Instead, we have settled for half-measures. Wittgenstein told us 'Whereof we cannot speak, thereof one must be silent.' Freud said we must relegate everything we can't understand to the unconscious. We can apprehend what is hidden only when it leaks out as a symptom or psychotic episode. Psychology backs up the claim that there is a limit. It says we can stay sane only by repressing or sublimating what we cannot comprehend. Beyond this limit we break down.

But classical philosophy won't settle for this defeatism. It contends that humans are capable of understanding everything. It challenges the very idea of limitation. It never stops digging deep into thoughts, feelings and behaviour. It says that recognition lies at the heart of humanity. 'Re-cognition' is the bringing back into the fold everything lost to thought. It says we can let all reality into our minds, ponder it, and then release it back into the world – without feeling guilty that we've let someone down, that there is something deeply odd about us, or that our feelings or thoughts are out of control. Classical philosophy offers a way forward by changing the rules of the game. It has the courage to ignore postmodernism's warnings against widening our intellectual horizons until we recognise that there is no limit. This means that it's scrutiny of the world is utterly stark and prescient. Philosophers care about what is happening around them, but they harden themselves against rebuke and say, 'apart from philosophy there is no method that is anything but partial.' Metaphysical abstraction may not seem to be immediately applicable to day-by-day human stresses. Yet philosophy is eventually able to resolve all things by stepping beyond humankind. It finds the unity of all things by placing its fulcrum in the universe. It says that we will never know humans until we enter into a conceptual process that leads us to the truth. Only then can we perspicaciously ask: What is it to be human?

The first philosophical questioning of the place of humans in the world may have been raised in a conversation between two great minds. One was Socrates, a man of the people, inveterate conversationalist, compassionate towards humanity, champion of the friendship, democracy and the Greek Agora (the open space in the city centre where people talked through all manner of things, including the governance of Athens). Socrates can be said to stand for philosophy. The other was Plato, consummate writer, thinker, and observer of others, interested in the play of the mind to the exclusion of virtually everything else, able to recognise his intellectual exceptionality and prepared only to engage with other exceptional minds, shy in social gatherings and doubtful of people's potential to find harmony amidst the barrage of myriad problems that disturb human relations. His only love was for Socrates. Plato can be said to stand for art. Thus art converses with philosophy, and the conversation immediately latches onto the question of society, of what happens when people come together. Plato was mortified by the death of his hero, mentor and (Platonic) lover, and couldn't understand how a society possessing such maturity, openness and perspicacity could kill someone so wise, caring and beneficent. Surely, he asked, Socrates' death reveals society to be empty and destructive when pressured by even the most disinterested of challenges. And yet Socrates loved

Athenian society and was prepared to engage with it where its nerves were most exposed and raw. Art and philosophy have pursued this conversation down to this day. They have not arrived at a conclusion. This book enters the conversation at a point where the relation between society and the human is intriguingly opaque.

Philosophy arose in Greece in response to the distress Sophocles describes in Thebes. It listened to the prevailing despair and realised that all our attempts to think and be moral or wise are superficial. It addressed itself to the forces that were bubbling over. It noticed the prevailing lack of a method with which to address them. Philosophy's response was to question every claim relentlessly. It can do this because it isn't an intellectual or academic discipline that delineates a tranche of knowledge. It doesn't possess a discipline-specific set of methods. It doesn't build theories. It is not an ideology or producer of dogma. In other words, it is not concerned with this opinion or that. What it does is involve people in a conversation that will break down all certainties. The point will be reached where, whatever their initial differences, people will realise they are travellers from a similar place. Philosophy is the audience to the world; it is not another actor. It is not subject to the human gaze because it adopts a vantage point outside the human. It doesn't practise any of the intellectual methods available because it is method itself. That is, by questioning everything remorselessly, it makes totality its yardstick. Thinking pivots to the absolute - to truth, reality, infinity, totality and God – but doesn't arrive there because that would be a position. Merely pivoting thought towards the absolute loosens all the intellectual stanchions. The power of critique cuts through all claims to knowledge, determinacy or certainty. Philosophy is not concerned with studying truth or reality; it does not think about them. Instead it removes clutter from the mind that blocks connection to them. The pivoting of the fulcrum of the mind beyond the human to reality makes philosophy a meta-method able to search for the truth that lies behind all mental constructs. It realises that, unless humans are understood against the backdrop of totality, they become an echo chamber of the mind.

Plato asked philosophical questions of the pain he saw all around him. This led him to question the language we bring to bear on our daily dealings. For example, a remark like 'I feel angry' will be sure to touch our and other's moral and emotional nerve-ends. But when abbreviated to a simple 'I feel,' the remark has even greater power. It can now shift semantic tectonic plates and multiply philosophical possibilities. This is because the phrase 'I feel' transforms what was a personal expression of experience into an enquiry into the nature of feelings. By removing the predicate 'angry' I remove what obstructs my connection to totality. The predicate has specified which feelings I have; yet, how can I possibly be so specific? Am I not telling myself what I feel and making it personal as well? Am I not drawing on customary social thinking to specify my feelings? All I can say for sure is that

I feel. This claim makes clear my commonality with others. To say 'I feel' shows how far I've absorbed everything that I connect to in others. Feelings pass back and forth like energy impulses. Indeed, they show that there is no me! This move has returned us to the wellspring of philosophy, the search for universal truth. It shows that thinking that acknowledges the interrelationship of things tells us more about humans than any attempt to draw deep meaning from singular personal experiences. Lacking the context of totality, appeals to our experience do not reveal how much we, the ones experiencing, are involved in the matter at hand. Kant told us we can't know that people are individually recognisable. It is for this reason that this book uses two Greek methods to explore the human - firstly, dialectics as a non-confrontational, conversational move (seeing the other side of an argument) that releases a mind from the prison of self, and secondly, the conjoining of the immaterial with the material in a move towards totality that we have come to call metaphysics. And, following the classical lead, to avow that everything about the human can be explained by reference to what happens when humans come together. These methods have been applied to all that is said on the following pages.

The book looks at 11 claims to be avatars of the human. I treat each in turn. But I also divide them into two groups. The first group explains the human from the point of view of a socially-constructed self. This explanation holds centre ground today. The second group asks about the human once it has dispensed with the self. This latter move powerfully disturbs the modern mind. Yet the Greeks put it at the centre of their philosophy. They also realised that the degree of equanimity achieved in one's daily life depends on the extent to which the question of non-self is explored. And, that this demands a lot of courage. The Greeks considered this to be the ultimate test for the human project.

The book falls into three Parts. Part One looks at ideas that arose during the Axial Age of c800BC to c200AD. These ideas are the basis of western philosophy and they underpin this book. The Greeks subscribed to a monist view of things, an idea of inclusivity that embraces everything, even splits and dichotomies, without itself becoming divided. The Greeks contended that all we need do initially is to clear our minds of suppositions and then whatever we see will be real. With a clear mind our thoughts can soar into the universe. The Greeks achieved this overview by taking a 'God's eye view' of the human. To bridge dichotomies they had always to see the other side of an argument. This is where their love of talking was an immense benefit. As epitomised by Socrates, they would converse exhaustively with anyone who was prepared to join in with them. But in modern times monism struggles to find a forum. Humans have 'swallowed' the universe; the personal mind is made to act as a micro-universe. When a person meets another they bring their personal universe along with them. They have nothing outside themselves to share.

Part Two looks at what happens when humans are preoccupied with themselves. Self-regard expresses itself in a focus on being, the generation and expression of feelings, family, society and a force that can presently be called the socio. Human self-preoccupation has pushed metaphysics to the margins.

But, as Part Three shows, the concept of monism has not disappeared. Here I switch attention back to approaches that acknowledge a more direct debt to the Greeks. Their concern with reality allowed them to observe human existence from the point of eternity. This move convinced them that conceptualisation and human liberation grow from the same root. Nietzsche echoed this point when he called for future philosophers to be psychologists. He wanted philosophy to engage with daily human struggles. Plato and his nemesis Nietzsche were united in treating philosophy as an activity that turned philosophers into players in the game. Philosophy has built a platform from which we can start to unravel the riddle of the Sphinx.

A NOTE ON METHODOLOGY

Enquiries about humans have thus far been more concerned with studying them than with engaging with them in and of themselves. But the Greeks approached things differently. They understood that the knowing of the human cannot be separated from a direct engagement with it, that we cannot ask universal questions from some neutral or academic vantage point. This is difficult to comprehend for a mind steeped in postmodernism. Indeed, the questioning of the place of self or experience in the grand scheme of things has almost died out in recent times. Yet the Greeks devised a method to deal with this aspect of mind: they looked to the dialectical to and fro of conversation to carry thought beyond the conversationalist's own sense of self or personal experience. The opening of the mind to a vantage point anchored outside the self provides the foundations for the making of metaphysical theories of the universe.

The Greeks spoke a language of wholeness, not of fragmentation. They were concerned with humanity in the round as it revealed itself in the cauldron-heat generated by large, interactive gatherings. The phrase 'large gatherings' should not be taken to apply to a football crowd, political rally, large workforce, or suchlike – these gather for a specific purpose from which the group draws its collective identity. Instead I mean gatherings that enhance individual liberty – firstly, by exposing us to direct engagement with radically different people (those we usually avoid) and secondly, by opening our minds to grand ideas that have the power to loosen the grip of the self. In these ways the opening of our minds permits us to accept more and more about the human that would otherwise lie hidden. It may seem ironic to suggest that individual liberty arises when we move freely in the 'ontological void' of reality. Yet this is what the Greeks were saying. However outside metaphysics or the Greek version of dialectics, modern and postmodern enquiries into humanity seek to anchor the human in the 'I' or 'me,' in specific personal human needs, preferences, identities, affiliations, and so on. Humankind has certainly been discussed in broad terms - as an evolutionary or developmental phenomenon arising in nature, as an issue of public order in the work of Michel Foucault, or as a critique of humanism like John Gray's *Straw Dogs*, for example. But these studies are concerned with analyses of trends, descriptions and dispositions, or with relations between aspects, properties, qualities or parts. In other words, they take a human-centric view that leads to the fragmenting of wholeness.

The gift of mind has inevitably attracted the attention of students of theories of mind. This branch of philosophy assumes that humans are concrete beings that operate under rules of cause and effect, and that they possess a nature akin to that of animals and plants. Understandably the mind has also attracted students from the philosophical sub-branch of being. Their point of departure is Heidegger's Ontological Turn. But in recent years doubt has been cast on the validity of the epistemology-ontology relationship. The terms are too heavily dependent on each other for them to stand in their own right. Moreover philosophy's treatment of the human since the classical era has settled on its 'nature,' on humanity's inability to engage with reality, and on the improvement of the lot of humans. In other words, the notion of the totality of the human awaits deconstruction; it remains a bundle of theories, surmises and assumptions. Notions and theories that allude to only part of the totality of a human are allowed to pass for the whole of it. The core of the individual human has yet to find its place in seamless, unbounded reality. For this reason I treat all approaches outside metaphysics and Greek dialectics as anthropomorphic, that is to say, they consider the universe to be serving human needs. They fail to put the human back into the universe.

I focus on the big questions that only metaphysics asks. Ironically these questions connect us directly to the existential dilemmas that fill our daily lives, to the moods, dreads, hopes and fears of a soulful existence. Yet, the deepest irony, metaphysics reveals the faulty underpinning of our thinking about these 'experiences.' It points to the dichotomous thought that divides our moods into bright or dark. Philosophy's engagement with big ideas avoids falling into this trap. The very scale of the questions precludes a slide into asking which side is right or wrong, or who wins and who loses. Accordingly this book does not seek an 'outcome' such as a better model or explanation. Rather, it sets out to remove the clutter that obstructs our thinking about the human.

I rely heavily on three methods. Firstly, I place absolute ideas such as reality, truth and God at the centre of the investigation. Yet, I do not mean the settling on an absolute, which would amount to the taking up of a position. This would stop the flow. I mean moving towards the absolute; this movement is enough to unblock congestion of thought so it can again roam where it will. We are familiar with the human tendency to start a conversation by adopting a position or by standing on one side of a binary divide. However classical philosophy hones in on the permanence and totality of things. It thereby tests the claims of particulars, like a self or personal experience, to be whole in themselves by pitching these claims against an absolute. Absolutes are totalities: they reveal the inadequacy of a name, identity or signifier that cannot engross the whole of the entity it names. Indeed, as an opening move, classical thought treats the idea of an individual person as lacking ontological status. This is because personhood is based on two fallacious claims. The first is a belief in the experiences we claim to have; the interior argument. The second is a reliance on what others say about us, the exterior argument. Both remain in the territory of epistemology because they arise from within the investigation itself. They remain inside the mind of the observer. To be sure, the individual human body has been granted ontological status. It is the substantial part of a human, the part that connects it to nature. But we can go much further than this and use this ontological claim as the basis of a new hypothesis. Classical thinking encourages us to start an enquiry in this way. We can move our thought processes forward by transferring the body's claim to ontological status onto a fictional, universal 'body' that we will call wholeness. Now the individual human becomes a second move, something once-removed from the whole. The status of all claims to speak from a personal vantage point - when I say I think, feel or experience, and what others think and feel about me - are now highly questionable. I will use this method in subsequent pages to test all claims to totality.

The second Greek method I adopt is the idea of a 'fulcrum' of thought. The Greeks placed the fulcrum outside the self. This idea takes the weight of selfhood off our shoulders. It helps us make broader sense of the personal cross we think we bear. When there is trouble we blame ourselves or point the finger at someone else. Astonishingly we never blame the idea. And yet Plato told us that behind every interpretation or appearance is an idea we would do well to investigate. Ideas are universal. So, by moving the fulcrum of our thinking outside ourselves we gain a vantage point in eternity. This move is reflected in our use of language. When for example I say 'I want to be happy' and emphasise 'I' and 'happy,' I miss the point that 'want' is the fulcrum, verb or operative word that holds subject and object together. The verb is our route back to the universe. Yet we rarely use it in this way. The early Greeks warned us that human distress occurs when we rely on unexamined intellectual constructions. It occurs too when we treat our unexamined sense-perceptions as reality. These moves persuade us to give authority to those with prominent profiles - high achievers and celebrities. We then believe we fall short of them or, worse still, live through them. Our process of thinking starts to give way if we take our eye off the fulcrum. Ironically, our first move is usually genuine and insightful: when we contemplate an idea we quickly see the cracks in it. Yet, as we see through it, our relation to it changes. The same applies as we get closer to people. We say: 'I love you and want to get to the essence of you. But you are not what you claim you are.' Yet we are surprised when the intensity we bring to the search ruins everything. We have not yet realised that humans desire to desire and not to desire happiness, intimacy or anything else (whatever they actually say). Our capacity to love and commit to each other is wonderful. But what has happened is that we've taken our eye off the ball. The ball is the fulcrum of thought. Moving it outwards to the world allows us to observe things without merging with them. This is the inestimable value of the idea of the fulcrum.

The third method brings together two idea – the 'within' and the 'in-between.' We must remember that philosophy is an activity that projects thinking beyond the mind. Accordingly it shifts attention from the energy produced by the solipsism of personal thought (the within) to the invigorating forces that arise from rigorous exchanges with diverse others (the in-between). The within is that which is already deemed coherent and socially or logically acceptable. It is established thinking. Its energy is contained inside the solitary self. But the solitary self needs to connect to something outside itself if it is to comprise more than its arbitrary boundaries. The within can certainly be said to reflect a meta 'out-with.' But Hegel suggests that it will remain a reflection until dialectical movement incorporates it into another thing or force. The within is a settling for partial understanding. The energy generated there doesn't lack intensity. But it tends to be narrow, fantastical, repetitive, and to rehearse social nostrums. From a want of security, it produces thinking that stays close to what people in general are already thinking.

On the other hand, the in-between produces an abundant, centrifugal, entropic energy from encounters with others. These encounters force us to consider what we might otherwise have found inconvenient or distasteful. Differences, disjunctions and disturbances abound as the philosopher strives to bring into the light what has been kept hidden, avoided or disapproved of. Plato says that what we see around us is the shadow of an idea. Similarly monism tells us that everything has its place in the universe. Metaphysics is an incorporative move; it embraces all that is other, dissonant and fractious. It deals with what happens when open-minded people come together and generate the energy of the in-between.

These three methods provide the cutting edge of the explorations that follow. The 'view from eternity' opens the mind to the most revealing ideas, ideas capable of endless change. It tests to destruction all claims to be the avatar of the human that are based on parts, shadows or simulacra of the whole. The Greeks understood the place of humans to rest in reality or totality; nowhere else. But reality is infinite and consciousness seems to have a life of its own. Lacking a nature and disconnected from instinct, humans are adrift. Accordingly the book doesn't go in search of an anchor for humans, whether in reality or anywhere else. Classical thought tells us we are real already. In the following pages I will enquire into that which suborns us into believing we are real, that which has been masquerading as reality. Reality lies behind it.

PART ONE: IN THE BEGINNING

CHAPTER ONE: EXPULSION FROM NATURE

'All of us, in our human and realised life, are but the caricatures of our soul. We are always less than what we are. We are always a grotesque translation of what we wished to be, of what we inwardly and truly are.' Fernando Pessoa.

The moment we humans realised we possessed a mind was the moment we were expelled from nature. We were no longer confined by animal nature. At most we might be said to have a half-nature. Our minds detach us from a life lived wholly through the senses. We can no longer be ourselves because the proclivity of the mind to reflect on itself throws everything about us, including our thinking, into question. We have shed who we are (animal) and become who we are not (immaterial; idea). At its most elementary, the human dilemma can be said to arise from body-mind dualism. We are both in the world as an animal and outside it as a thinker - at the very same time. Yet, also at the same time, we struggle to handle the fact that our consciousness distinguishes between entities while our bodies remain more or less the same. We seek to compensate for the instability caused by our dependence on the mind by constructing an identity that will give us a unitary presence in the world. But attempts to grasp at certainty by gaining social recognition fail because our identities are fluid: we copy only too felicitously those whom we love or admire. When we join a society, community, institution or nation in a desperate search for an identity or sense of belonging we start to think consensually and the spark of consciousness dies. Society strives to make our thinking mutually exclusive; thinking then regresses to the mean. Education, family life, culture and the media offer no help with these matters and life begins to feel meaningless. We have detached from reality in an attempt to rid ourselves of the problematic aspects of the gift of consciousness. We thereby fail to explore the mind's power to conceptualise the gap between us and reality and we find we have thrown the baby out with the bathwater. And yet, as Descartes told us, thinking is where humans start. By extension, I venture, it is the only way forward for humankind.

What does it mean, to gain a mind and be expelled from nature? It is clearly more than a simple calculation of gain and loss. We've gained consciousness and its attendant power of reasoning and imagination, but this has brought in its train the superego and depression. We've lost touch with our bodies, the visceral and the id, but in any case their immediacy and forcefulness frighten us. Is then the outcome lose-lose? Heidegger says we were thrown into an existing unwelcoming world; from the nothing of reality into the world which we know as something. His view played a large part in creating a postmodern obsession with human exceptionality and alienation. But Plato says we were thrown out of the world into nothingness. So the issue revolves around what we mean by something and nothing. In *Less Than Nothing* Slavoj Zizek takes up Hegel's challenge and reverses the Pre-

Socratic question (how does something come from nothing?) and asks: How can nothing come from something? Zizek takes nothingness to be reality, and reality to be nature, the body, or the visceral. 'Something' is now the bundle of mental constructs that fills our thinking. In other words, Plato's 'return' to reality is blocked by mental constructs. So, a belief in the possession of a discrete mind becomes a problem when we leave it unattended. It will intercede between us and reality and persuade us there is something. But this something is appearance, a simulacrum or a figment of the mind. Thus a return to reality from a world entangled in somethingness involves the strictest questioning of the way we think. The Greeks understood that to realise we are already real involves the letting go of both the self and its attendant inner life. The urge to treat humans as exceptional, mysterious and wanting will then go. To be given a mind and to be expelled from nature did not make the human a failure; it made it possible for humans to become harmonious with all things on a level not available to animals. It raised the bar as never before. It is a win-win situation! Postmodernism's preoccupation with human alienation has blinded us to this opening. On later pages I am mindful of the possibility that humans can become harmonious with themselves and the world.

A Greek myth recounts how two Titan brothers Prometheus and Epimetheus brought about the human Fall from Grace. The brothers were told by the gods to populate the earth with animals and humans. But

Epimetheus (Greek: after-thought) had favoured the wellbeing of other animals by giving them feathers for wings and strong legs and jaws. This left humans vulnerable, so his brother Prometheus (Greek: forethought) sought to correct the imbalance. He did this by making humans stand upright and giving them fire he had stolen from heaven. His reward was to be condemned to perpetual torment. Why this was so is a puzzle. Maybe Zeus, the chief god, was angry because he liked to play with simple-minded humans. Maybe the power of fire presaged a human future that would forever carry the millstone of technology round its neck. Maybe the gods treasured their monopoly of physical energy. But a more challenging explanation is that Prometheus wanted human affairs to be forever free of mystery, to be forever perfect. Prometheus went too far. He ignored the Greek insight that to hit the mark we must know where to stop, to be just good enough. His correction condemned humans to a life of aspiration, to be forever striving after perfection. Humans no longer lived like other animals and yet nonetheless they were torn apart by dissatisfaction.

Philosophy offers a version of this story, but takes it much further. In place of fire there is consciousness. We start with a meeting between a thinker and an object of thought that splits the conscious person apart. The thinker is not clear if what he thinks is a thought or the object of that thought. The meeting confuses the thinker, creating panic. Here is the dilemma posed by

Prometheus' extravagant gift. And yet, we can say that there is no overriding need to oppose consciousness to nature; consciousness is itself a divine spark. It can transcend nature and connect us to the primordial. Integration occurs when we place consciousness (or God) in a close relation to nature a la Spinoza. Indeed philosophy is very capable of putting the consciousness-nature split aside and engaging directly with the human. Our entry point is consciousness itself. It is a wonderful gift. But because society will not take up classical philosophy's method, consciousness goes haywire. This may explain why it has been postulated that we use consciousness barely five percent of the time.

We can use the mind to pursue the cosmic vibrations, cooings or resonances that our longing creates. But the attempts made so far have only had the effect of pushing longing deeper underground. Freud placed it in the unconscious, which itself constitutes a pining for something lost. His move has drawn attention away from consciousness into the nether regions of the soul and has led to a prolonged focus on what is hidden to the mind. Existentialism famously attempts to find something that it claims underpins humankind. John Caputo points out that our attempt to connect to God by using His name merely confines us within the mind. Yeshayahu Leibowitz has pushed the argument for cosmic connectivity beyond breaking point. He claims that expulsion from paradise is final: there is no way back for humans. We have had no nature since the Garden of Eden. But, it can be argued that these explanations, valuable as they are, hesitate on the brink of the gap between humans and the world. Were these thinkers to peer into the gap they would find a cornucopia of impulses that generate life, animation and movement. And further, they would see that living with a daily sense of something missing diverts us from understanding that the search for life is the object itself. Certainly a search for meaning needs something to pitch itself against, the more so when meaning itself doesn't exist and will never appear. The issue becomes a matter of faith. In other words, Leibowitz puts God to one side in order to elevate faith itself. God is now the epitome of thinking. And thinking is geared to the pursuit of the object of faith. This means that, as one thinks, there is God. So there is nature of a kind, a nature which has no nature. It derives from Aristotle's telos. As we search for nature a meta-nature emerges. As we stand before God (as thought) we feel a striving that Leibowitz calls the will. This connects us to each other and inspires us to extraordinary acts of magnanimity.

Leibowitz takes God to be transcendent: 'God did not reveal Himself in nature or in history.' (1) But, if we metaphorically bring God inside the human, we arrive at the idea of consciousness. Because humans lack an anchor in nature they find that an internalisation of consciousness makes it impossible to know who they are. Something always throws everything into question and annihilates that which promises to keep the fixtures in place. We are aware of some sort of cosmic cooing or background noise but can't connect to it. The noise cannot be articulated; it doesn't appear in our conversations.

So, our task is to find the spark. I define it as an entity that recognises itself, that doesn't work against itself. We can approach it by reference to the rise of monotheism during the Axial Age. It heralded the end of idol-worship. Attention switched from matter to ideas (or the soul), from what the senses told us about things to what we thought about things. Mind was now considered a better connoisseur of reality than the senses. Essence was associated not with physicality or an image of matter but with the idea of it. The idea of the soul took hold. We can take these moves further by converting the energy generated by the trembling of the soul into a drive to enquire. This move anchors thought and anchors us in thought. Our direction of travel is towards the mystery that lies at the heart of all things. It has appeared as the concept of becoming in Plato; as God-as-nature in Aristotle and Spinoza; as the idea of development at the centre of recent scientific research; and as the notion of process at the heart of systems theory. It invites us to approach thought from an unusual angle. It asks us not to be concerned with what we observe but to ask what we can infer from what we observe. This move points towards essence. It asks not what a thing is but what it is becoming. We have returned to Plato.

The philosopher understands God as an idea. Leibowitz's way of dealing with this move is to say that God doesn't care about us, but we cannot do without Him. God is outside both the universe and meaning. He is the cosmic means of communication, responsibility and loving. We are in pursuit of Him because He takes us not to subject, object or reality but to humankind before reality. It is becoming clear that it is not God we are pursuing ultimately but the pursuit itself. The move is itself a reorientation from fixity towards the renewal of movement.

CHAPTER TWO: THE STARTING POINT: THE AXIAL AGE
'In the new ideologies of the Axial Age, therefore, there was a general agreement that human life contained a transcendent element that was essential.' Karen Armstrong, *A History of God*.

The Axial Age (c800BC to c200AD) revolutionised humanity's understanding of its place in the universe. No longer were we forced to accept the world as a product of our own minds. Up to that point, the mind's internal mechanism forced thinking to pass through the lens of personal identity. Now it became possible to gain a full understanding of the human by casting the fulcrum of thought outside the human altogether. Logos - conceptual thought - allowed humans to appreciate the richness of the world by tapping into the full force of consciousness.

At the same time, the Axial Age in Greece questioned the prevailing view that humankind was governed by incomprehensible forces. The Greeks considered the physical evolution of human beings to be secondary to the development of their mental capacities. Lacking any prior determination, humankind was now free to go where angels feared to tread. The Greeks were saying that humanity's failure to hold a fixed place in the universe is actually a gift in disguise. By possessing a mind humans can become whatever they conceive themselves to be. Such trusted nostrums as sanity and goodness are revealed as human constructs. Agency, it was conceived, lies in the universe, not in humans. Assumptions derived from human judgement are deemed faulty until subjected to philosophical deconstruction. The jocular exhortation to pull yourself up by your own bootstraps illustrates this point. Where a literal mind might reply: it cannot be done, the Axial Age philosopher might reply: do it anyway. Everything is in the asking.

History tells us how the human spirit has developed thus far. But philosophy is a thought experiment that asks what it might eventually look like. The Greek idea of hubris - seeking to emulate a god - changed from a punishable offence to the preferred life for a philosopher. Earlier peoples were kept in the dark about the nature of things, but a search for knowledge became de rigueur in the Axial Age. Nothing was accepted at face value: burgeoning views about a good life treated custom and habit with disdain. A Greek of the new disposition might have asked why anyone would seek friends who are similarly disposed when acute differences are so powerfully attractive. These thinkers revelled in the strange melange of companions life throws across our path. They acknowledged that the soul derives succour from the unknown. They might have exhorted us to step out of line more often. Socrates was convinced that, as things stood, families were organised as friendship-repulsing projects. Moreover he was aware of an incestuous link between family and society that stifled human freedom in its birth pangs. Family stood for patriarchy, unchanging roles and rules, and the dictatorship of romantic love. Friendship stood for unlimited pursuit of ideas, the swapping of roles, for minimal rules beyond an aversion to physical violence, for equality between friends. It challenges the parental authority that dominated families. It offers the prospect of a family upending parental authority and becoming a community of siblings. Beyond everything else Socrates wanted human freedom for the citizenry of Athens. Family led to inward-looking-ness and personal secrets, silence over the biggest issues, an obligation to demonstrate love and care in ritualised ways towards other family members, and an authoritarian approach to governance of both family and state. The only hope for Athens, as he saw it, was to produce citizens who would question everything, venture outside social rules, and celebrate reality as a wonderful space in which to engage with others. He was not inherently anti-family, but he demanded that this institution be subjected to philosophical enquiry like anything else on the principle that nothing is sacrosanct in philosophy. He prioritised the approval of frank, whole-hearted friends above social recognition. Friends encouraged us to ignore the seduction of status and of a material reward system backed by a rigid institutional ethos. Staying true to ourselves, Greek thinkers might have said, eclipses the rewards of status conferred by conformity. As the stanchions of society loosened, democracy became a platform for change. The ability of a conservative world order to hold the burgeoning ideas and viewpoints together was thrown into doubt. It dawned on a growing number of people that harmony was robust enough to accommodate fractious humankind within the great scheme of things. The Axial moment witnessed a once-and-for-ever breakthrough. There has never been its like since.

Out of this revolution emerged a new notion of the human. No longer controlled by a warrior code of honour, social custom or superhuman intervention, humankind pondered the idea that there are now no limits to what a human can become. Plato's contention that all things physical or emotional are anchored in an idea gave birth to the notion of human freedom. The Axial revolution revealed that the human capacity to think without flinching allows us to make sense of everything, even the most apparently inchoate or mystical. As the tectonic plates shifted, unsuspected and yet thrilling juxtapositions of ideas saw the light of day. Appearances no longer served as a guide to reality. In this shifting landscape fortitude became a sine qua non for those seeking to stay true to themselves. The Greeks considered courage to be the supreme virtue. Its application could change an endurable life into an adventurous one.

We always yearn for a good life. But before we ask how it is constituted we must ask: what is a life? And before we do that we have to ask: what is a human? The good life and the human are interrelated issues because the human gift of thought has to be used wisely if thinking is not to destroy us. These are strong words. But once we let the quality of our thinking sink beneath a certain level, our grasp of the movement of the world is insufficient to protect us against its depredations. It is unsurprising then that the central focus of philosophy has always been the conundrum of humanity. When homo sapiens was given a mind it was given a double-edged sword. The merest deviation from a point of equilibrium can turn the mind from a force that elevates us to one that ruins us. The visceral animal body is always pulling us down to unreflective physical motion whereas our elastic consciousness experiences us totally differently: rebelling against the purely physical it pulls us upwards to a parallel world moved by inspiration and wonder. It is in this latter world that we can be whatever we want. Yet this thought attracts and frightens us in equal measure, forcing humans to search for a 'human nature' in the brain or the genes; assigning responsibility to hard-wiring rather than to happenstance or human will. When we find the courage to hold ourselves to the sticking post the mind will transport us to magnificence beyond our wildest dreams. But the pull downwards is always waiting to assert itself. Our sensitivity, compassion and imagination draw us into the lives of others and into complexities and dead ends to the point that we keep getting hurt. A person can for a while go about life blissfully unaware that the wellbeing they take for granted hangs by a thread. One day a dear friend moves abroad, a partner packs their bags, or a job ends. In a moment, a life full of enriching encounters has become one of distanced pleasantries, of swapping of arid information, and of undemanding hobbies. Our imagination fails us. The soul wilts.

At this point we can either turn to a therapist or to philosophy. We are being reminded of something brutally simple: we can continue to live as if we need constant reassurance or we can start treating life as an adventure. As we slowly let go of pain, we might find ourselves asking a question so grand that it makes our personal experiences seem trivial: What is a human? What is this fractured, Janus-like state of affairs in which I live? How is it that I find myself teetering precariously on the divide between wonder and despair? How can I even begin to address an issue of this scale? The questions demand a philosophical response because only philosophy takes us beyond intellectual formulas and constructs to the freedom offered by concepts. Resort to formulas may be said to have caused the descent into distress in the first place. This book offers a philosophical response to questions provoked by humanity's reluctance to pivot towards the wonder of the world.

But we cannot start exploring until we tease out all the implications of Nietzsche's cri de coeur - future philosophers need to become psychologists. This is simply a re-statement of the old nostrum about thinkers being doctors of humankind. But it is saying more than that philosophers should take up a ministering role. A doctor was of course originally a teacher in the Socratic mould - someone who lived out the key thoughts and became a role-model for others. Crucially, when the Greeks referred to Socrates as a teacher, they meant he lived the philosophy he so fluently enunciated. Humans were diminished when philosophy lost psychology to the social-medical sciences. Philosophy became arcane, cloistered, a niche, dominated by men, and just one among many disciplines in university curricula across the western world from the mid-19th century. Metaphysics or dialectics - Aristotle's first philosophy - disappeared into specialised academic departments and lost its lived aspect.

So, the first move is to bring metaphysics and daily living back together again. Their interaction blossoms when humans relate. Now energy flows between people in myriad forms of relationship - love, the muse, the in-between, or the meta. (1) Only now can we address the Greek hypothesis that humans have no nature, that, like the ship of Theseus, we are forever reinventing ourselves, adding and subtracting components, until the only feature that remains from the original is a general term like 'ship' or, if it be a human, a personal name. The richness of human imagination is impossible to subsume into a concrete state or form. But if humans have no nature, what are they? Their dual capacity - animal and consciousness - makes it impossible for them to return to a simple animal state. The mind is an obstacle to thought because it thinks as a self about the manoeuvre that seeks to remove the self! We actually wish to remove a thought and yet our thinking about it entrenches the thought further. This is the dilemma of humankind. Animals almost invariably accept what their senses tell them. But classical thought tells us that when we think about a thing it comes into existence. The question then is: Dare we trust our thinking?

Today we are regressing to a pre-Axial state. We are asked to sacrifice ourselves for the greater good of institutions, organisations and ideologies. Hegel tells us nation rides above all else and that nation-building itself is subject to the rigours of time. Marx subsumes us in class. Freud tells us we must limit our aspirations to the sublimation of our passions. People are afraid to speak their minds for fear of legal retribution or public censure. Yet Axial Age thinking rested on the assumption that we need never fear negative repercussions from the pursuit of anything under the sun. Worked-through people already possess all the compassion and understanding needed to live in close proximity to each other. In other words, it is not individual miscreants who undermine society so much as the unwillingness of institutionalised society to allow people to be free. Nothing can actually upset the apple cart other than an attempt to keep it on a given path at any cost. Indeed, the Greeks would have said we do not do enough to pursue human magnificence, love or freedom. Because they were drawn to explore the great enigmas that humanity throws up, they might have added that our capacity to talk frankly about our deepest impulses and yearnings is what ultimately distinguishes us from other creatures. They believed that the soul aches for incorporation into a greater whole, and that philosophy rides on this idea, not on logic or science or any attempt to signify, pin down or particularise.

The mind is a gift that requires the most careful cultivation. The gap it creates between a subject and an object is impossible to bridge. But the reason for this is that the gap is a mind construct. Invariably, the result will be that we, the subject, will try harder and harder until we give up and reject the prospect of bridging altogether. The gap threatens our mental and emotional equilibrium. It forces our thought inwards where it becomes self-referential. Only when we realise that the very move towards otherness, call it love or desire, yearning or exploring, is itself intimacy; only then will we realise that making direct contact with a particular person or object is an illusion. Our very reaching out to the world is enough: it taps into the process that moves the world. We need do no more. Only now can we let go of the dream of connection and realise that connection to the world is an idea, a conceptual move. We can begin to realise that what we want to connect to is love, not that to which we attach love. When we are honest we can admit that this can be to almost anyone or anything. Love is now the fulcrum of thought. This fulcrum is not in our personal mind but in consciousness. It is outside us. From this vantage point the world gazes at us, at humanity. Imaginative thinking has revealed the gap between humanity and the world to be a cornucopia of conceptual possibilities instead of a chasm to be bridged. Subject and object fade away before the penetration of thought. The 'I' who views it from this side and the particularity, whether person or thing, which is perceived to be on the other side, pale into insignificance. All constructed thought arises out of consideration for human sensibility. Now it can be jettisoned. Abstract thinking takes us to a firmament of absolutes like truth, beauty, reality and God. Greek thinkers were convinced that there is nothing to be gained from the acquisition of knowledge of things. This is but a chimera. We can use the mind imaginatively only when we stop obsessing about things and realise that all our worries are about matters of appearance that hide more substantial issues. Only then will a space emerge in which concepts can be born.

At this point thinking changes - this is the Axial moment. It shows for instance that concepts that tell us about reality are hollow. This 'about' treats the concept as a substitute for reality, implying that reality is actually out there somewhere and that the concept is the nearest we can get to it. The Greek message is different. It is unapologetically stark: reality just is a concept, nothing more. It is never about something. It is it. There are only ideas. It follows that humans are ideas too. It is not a question of whether or not an idea like reality can anchor the human. It is about our ability to use ideas. This is the real challenge of the Axial Age.

CHAPTER THREE: THE HUMAN AND REALITY.

'Platonism is, what the doctrine of Socrates never was, a system of the world, embracing that whole province of external Nature from which Socrates had turned away to study the nature and the end of man.' Francis MacDonald Cornford, *Before and After Socrates*.

People seem forever to want to connect to other people or things, or even themselves. They cannot accept that recognising they are alone, and that this will not change, is the first move towards reality. This acceptance is only another way of describing the process of individuation. Yet people never give up; they'd change reality, if we could, in order to connect to others. But the desire to change reality misunderstands reality itself. It is already constant change. This is its consistency, as Heraclitus told us. So why would we seek to change change itself? The urge to connect seems to arise from a wish for knowledge, for a wish to satisfy our restless minds. But we project the devil into what we don't know, into the dark side of the moon, so to speak. A desire for connection arises from our unknowing. Heraclitus suggests that humans find their place in the flux of reality. But what does this mean? It means we must look beyond the human and its desire to construct a self if we are to understand humans. The construction of a self is an attempt to create a unitary entity that commands its own destiny. But the implication of Heraclitus's insight is that human essence lies in human connection to everything.

Yet everything is an overflowing cornucopia, not an object. It cannot be connected to. But the self is never satisfied; it keeps trying. It wants one-on-one connection. It is in response to this dilemma that the concept of 'otherness' arose. An encounter with another reveals the connection to all things that the self is trying to deny. But of course, otherness is not containable; it is everything that is not me. So long as we don't turn it into an entity or object it serves our purpose. It stands for the indeterminacy of the universe. When we realise that this kind of connection or immersion makes a mockery of the barriers of the self we are on a journey, not to reality or totality as absolutes, but to the formlessness of thought that an unexamined mind abhors. Interconnection, otherness and the in-between are ideas that connote a space or nexus where animation emerges; they are zones the self cannot access. In the rest of this book all claims to be the avatar of the human will be examined in the light of this Greek insight.

As ever, the problem is the mind. What we mistake for it, and what fills it, is content. This arises when we treat appearances seriously. And the biggest appearance of all is the self. We are already real; we do not need to construct an edifice out of the bricks and mortar of social attributions. Indeed, we do not need to go in search of reality, as if it is out there somewhere beyond us. In other words, we do not need to give attention to the appearance of the world or ourself because reality pertains when we evacuate the contents of our mind.

Nothing else needs to be done. Reality is the process or movement of ideas that fills a mind emptied of content.

The problem emerges when we look out on the world. We objectify it and at the same time we objectify our internal registering of it. We take this internal registering to be us. All our terrors derive from it. It is this that needs to be removed. Plato's 'return' is not a return of humans to reality – we are already there! – but of all this content back to the world whence it came. Reality now reveals itself as the endless processing of ideas, and life is the ideas that pass through our unblocked minds. We do not need to try and recognise reality. Indeed, we cannot. Use of the unfettered mind is recognition. So, there is no need to anchor ourselves in reality. This is an oxymoron. All we need do is to anchor outside ourselves that which we mistakenly took to be ourselves.

A number of questions arise from this move: Is that which emerges in my mind me? Am I a priori to all thought? Am I distinct from my thoughts and feelings? A common reply can be given to all these questions. It is that I am that which reflects on my thoughts and feelings. This is Plato again. His return is not of humans to the world, but the opposite. That which is not us returns to the world, leaving us as pure process, thinking and reflection. Only then can we recognise that our gaze can turn everywhere without restriction. Nothing about us is fixed. In other words, everything we mean by God is a projection of what we have not yet accepted about ourselves.

The Greeks bequeathed us a formidable insight: humans do not need to be tortured by the mind. The idea of mind tells us that we can go beyond experience. If however we attempt to make mind and reality relate one-on-one, in other words without reflecting on this divide, we (mind) will latch onto the object of observation (reality) and either fuse with or be antagonistic to it. We need only think of the difficulty of relating intimately to another person when there is no facilitative third force in the offing. Accordingly Plato told us to look at the mind and understand it - otherwise we will be stuck. The problem is that we can no longer be an animal and yet we have not fully freed ourselves of all we associate with being an animal. We are in limbo, in a state of evolutionary arrest. We haven't yet learned that we can handle the workings of our minds as easily as we can control the movement of our fingers.

To understand mind we must detach from it (stand under it). If we stay in the mind we cannot parent the thoughts that arise; we are too involved with them. However, once the mind is returned to the world, the primordial yearning to belong is satisfied. We can understand the world and all things in the round. But if we do nothing, mind, which hasn't yet learned to reflect on things overall, will talk to itself. The irony is that, if we take the great philosophical project to be the integration of the mind into the world, we must now split the mind - one part becoming a mini-mind capable of observing things, the other part being returned to the world. The part that goes back to the world is the one filled with content. The content is returned to the world from whence it came. I am treating the content-filled mind here as biological, as instinct or intuition. It can return to the world because it is not reflective. What is left as the mind proper is reflection, meta-thought. This can now reach beyond the world of physics or biology. It can ontologise ideas.

The mind-reality split is replicated in the human sphere in the form of the Freudian id-superego divide. We fear fusing with another; we come close, pull back, and then equivocate. This can cause acute distress. There is no connection and yet desire for connection is great and unsatisfied. We envy the immediacy of nature and the life of simple animals which appear to be free of these dilemmas. Again the mind is the cause. The problem arose in Plato. He told us that an understanding of mind would resolve all our issues - and then he himself hesitated, not knowing where to go next. He wavered between telling us to return to reality and telling us to turn to the Forms (pure ideas or reflective mind). We have suffered from this faulty philosophy ever since. Indeed, it became a major weakness at the heart of psychological thought. Freud believed humans could achieve harmony, but only at the individual level, a limitation that can be traced all the way back to Plato. We can, Freud believed, progress from thesis (id) to antithesis (superego) and finally to synthesis (ego), but only as individuals. What this move ignores is the generative power that arises when people come together. The Greeks were fascinated by this power. Freud's view limits us because it holds us at the individual or animal level. The gathering together and intimacy of animals seem to be simple matters. But we are more than animals. The key issue is that a fear of engaging with others arises from a fear of engaging with other minds. This is what has bedevilled philosophy since Plato.

It becomes a second, academic move to ask what is reality. It is an idea or supposition that equates to totality, infinity, eternity, indeterminacy and potentiality. Bergson calls it the joining up of particularities that sustains eternity in every moment. It is not reducible to anything else and nothing lies outside it. Herein lies its integrity.

We can say of reality *that* it is, not *what* it is. The former statement recognises reality; the latter asks us to explain it. But it is inexplicable, unknowable. It is not there to fit our human criteria. When we attempt to define or explain it we are acting as if we are outside it. It is total, inevitable, unescapable, the absolute certainty of execution, emergence, and full impact. For reality just is. It embraces both Heraclitus' constant change and warfare between things and Parmenides' unchanging universe. It presupposes a state of indeterminacy, movement and entropy. And yet the constancy of its movement constitutes its permanence.

A few more things can be said about reality without waxing too poetical. It pulls all the strings. It seeps into every corner of life, including mind. Once one opens one's mind, reality emerges fully-formed, without compromise, partiality, incremental progression or false promise. There is something in reality that is generative, connective and assimilable. Reality has something in it that encourages things to intermingle. It unites all the elements that are aspects of it. It reaches out to us, always seeking to reveal itself. But its complexity and capacity for internal refraction mean that things are not necessarily what they appear. Many elements coexist, yet some are more salient than others. Indeed, its complexity can make it appear to us to be hiding or masking itself, to be revealing itself in fragments. To say these things is to recognise the meaning of totality, not to make an anthropomorphic statement.

When we particularise things by splitting them away from others we give way to a human desire to do, to meddle with reality. Seeking to do something suggests a failure to appreciate reality for what it is. The fault lies with the observer, not reality. All that needs noting is that the lens through which the observer observes has clouded up. This occurs when we prioritise ourselves at the expense of the world. We commonly ask: How am I feeling? But things would be different were we to ask: How are we, one and all, people in total, society at large, feeling? It must be remembered that nothing escapes the absolute or totality. Everything finds its place; humans no longer need to fight for their individual portion. However when we wallow in self-regard we force incoming reality to pass through a filter of our likes and dislikes. We might claim to be looking after our wellbeing. But we will have missed the crucial point that our wellbeing is at the mercy of forces beyond our control (other than temporarily). Ironically, by clutching at a sense of self, we make sure that much incoming reality passes us by. We may be proud of selecting the 'right' parts of reality to suit us. But personal experience is a poor guide to reality: it leaves out so much. How can we know what is best for us? To assume that we possess such knowledge places a heavy reliance on the prescience of the 'I.'

Two moves open the human to reality. Firstly, we can clear the mind of obstacles. Now, mind is on a par with reality in the sense that it is not foregrounded or subjected to the infinite regress of reflection. We can say that an anchoring, or return, of sorts has taken place at this point. But we must move on to the second stage in order to complete the move. The second stage is the falsification of the distinction between mind and reality. This allows us to make an outrageous pivot of thought - to treat both of them as appearance. It must be remembered that thus far we have been treating mind as biological, as being there from the start. But, when we treat it as appearance, the question is begged: Who now is the observer? The answer is: reflective mind or thought itself. This pivot possesses the extra virtue of resolving the issue of other minds. It does this because the splitting of mind is the birth of other minds. Generally people settle at the level of mind vs reality. But, when two people meet, things are not as simple as this binary divide implies. The mind (observer) can be denoted as the One that looks out on the Many of the other(s). 'Many' means the whole complexity of reality beyond me. But the observer, self or 'I' is not a unitary entity. The 'I' is a multiplicity. The release from the constraint of the simple mind-reality duality comes about when we see the 'I' as a One that already comprises Many. There are as many me's inside me as there are others outside me. Now the false division between unitary inner (mind) and multiple and complex outer (reality) gives way to a multiplicity of both. The second move makes clear to me that I don't know who I am: I am open to the full range of human possibility. We have generalised Freud's idea of personal individuation. I am now prepared to accept that everyone I know and all the things that people are capable of doing find an echo in me. But things don't stop there – as there is now no boundary between inner and outer worlds I am nothing other than an angle of perception.

We have returned to the key insight of the Greeks: the human is a response to or a processing of the energy that arises between people. Philosophy helps human encounters to engage with this energy by emptying the mind of obstructive content. It does this by returning the mind's internalisation of the world back to the world. Now we are able to think uninhibitedly. Now life as an unimpeded process can resume.

SUMMARY OF PART ONE

Part One places the challenges of the Axial Age on the table. Two stand out. Firstly, culture was about the narrativization of action before the Axial Age. Ideas were peripheral. The Axial thinkers broke this stranglehold by ontologising ideas. It was now possible to evolve the idea of reality. Given that reality is everything there is, the hypothesis that humans are real was but a short step further. Secondly, the ontologising of ideas presented a challenge to experience. For example, when I say I am hungry others usually concur with me without question because experience is deemed irrefutable. But now the idea of hunger creates a space between ideas and experience, a space that competes for our attention. When someone repeatedly makes claims from feelings or experience ('I,' 'mine') we are forewarned that the speaker is immersed in themselves. Narcissism is deemed a narrow, unstable basis for living. It can arise from an excess of mind; or from a wish to live as if the add-ons to life such as emotional atmosphere, titillation or drama are life itself. Whatever the reason, experience no longer vouchsafes credibility.

Once we reflect on experience in terms of excess its claims become disturbingly thin. Lacan's 'death of the signified' tells us that experience's claim to ground the human is now invalid: it involves an endless slide down a chain of signification. This slide distorts the effect that one mind has on another. Meetings of minds no longer take place against a backdrop of reality. Each speaks to the other from their own isolated experience, making an encounter impossible. Axial thinking did not discount the place of experience in life. But it wanted ideas to sit alongside experience so that experience could be reflected upon from an external fulcrum or objective point. Otherwise we will encounter, not the other, but a projection of the unexamined content of our own mind. Axial thinking placed the fulcrum outside ourselves in order for us truly to encounter each other. But it also meant that when we say we are real we are saying that our measure is the measure of all things. On the other hand, experience stays in the realm of appearance.

Another effect of the ontologising of ideas was to make indeterminable the place of humans in reality. Unexamined thinking will give us the impression we can hold thinking still, that we can stand outside reality. But Axial Age thinkers contended that we partake in reality's entropic flow, movement or flux. In order to partake we must first clear the mind (and then split it, in the way I outlined in the previous chapter).The reflective part of the mind can now conceptualise freely. Partaking is a process of manufacturing concepts and then returning to them as they develop through different stages of gestation.

The Greeks had little to say of reality itself. Reality just is. It is the human perspective on it that creates the mountains we force ourselves to climb and the phantoms with which we grapple. This is because consciousness makes us different. The ability to channel it ensures that we humans are not just a thing like a pebble. But we have handled consciousness badly: we struggle with what enters our minds. Accordingly we perceive reality to be fractured and relationship to others to be fraught. All attempts to resolve this dilemma fail. The Greeks considered that an attempt to engage directly with reality leads to mental derangement - to the terrors of fusion with another. The only approach to reality that avoids fusion while making it clear that simple contiguity is itself a matter of wonder is to admit we are real already. This requires that we return back to totality everything we have excluded from it. When we speak from the vantage point of a self we fail to recognise that we are omitting the non-self; we deny that we pay a heavy price for this narrowing of our perception. To open to non-self again we must clear our mind of suppositions. In other words, we must allow our mind the freedom to conceptualise. Then the logical impasses, binary divides and fracturing of reality that result from the play of mind can be reincorporated back into the world. The world, reality or totality is all-inclusive; it can incorporate these fractures without itself becoming fractured.

I've placed great emphasis on the Greek 'switch of vantage point.' It shows how, by letting go of the vantage point of the 'I,' we can adopt that of the observer. The 'I' imposes itself on the world; but the observer accepts the world on the world's terms. Put another way, the gaze of the self can only alight on another self or a fragment of reality. It is not capable of opening to wholeness. It views things from within the whole and so cannot include itself, the 'I,' in its range of view. Thus it is only capable of perceiving particularities and then only of approaching them judgementally. In contrast the observer perceives wholeness or totality. Fragmentation is now perceived merely to be hiding a relationship between the parts. Everything finds its place alongside and not in opposition to others. Whereas from the vantage point of wholeness the fragments relate to each other, from the vantage point of the self they are isolated and alienated.

It follows that a claim to certainty (such as an answer) is a fragment. It says: this far and no further. But a question opens things up by bringing back into consciousness what wasn't allowed before. By creating further thought a question creates the world anew. The Greek word dialogue means 'to go through the logos.' The trajectory of a new thought can be said to describe an arc that, before long, reaches a plateau as its energy wanes. At this point it starts to solidify into a construct, opinion, or an idee fixe. But a burst of inspiration can stimulate it to explore new ground. This was the effect of a Socratic interrogation. This forward-movement often disconcerts the thinker. It might lead to the state of mental disarray the Greeks called aporia. Fresh thoughts emerge out of the debris of old intellectual edifices. Thinking is free to engage with the world again, but a world without pre-ordained meaning.

We in the 21st century have grown fearful of meaninglessness. We've lost touch with the playfulness of the Greeks. They used ideas to lighten daily life. We are ill-served by the splitting of psychology from philosophy and the perception of psychology as the chief recourse in the handling of distress. We have forgotten the simple first step towards human wellbeing, which is to switch the vantage point of thinking from the self to the world. But psychology, and by extension society, still holds to the 'I.'

All of these points will be kept in mind as we examine five claims - being, feelings, family, society, and a force called 'the socio' - to be avatars of the human.

PART TWO: A MIND ABSORBED WITH HUMAN SUSCEPIBILITIES

CHAPTER FOUR: THE HUMAN AS A BEING

'Human reality is its own surpassing towards what it lacks; it surpasses itself toward the particular being which it would be if it were what it is.' Jean-Paul Sartre, *Being and Nothingness*.

The first claim I will examine is the idea of being (human *being*). It is used freely in common speech, but circumspectly in philosophy. I argue it is a problematic idea. Sartre's words above convey a sense of the problem. It has undergone a sea change since Greek times. Plato moved being or ontology away from its earlier association with substance (whence it was denoted as appearance) towards ideas, form or truth. Being was placed in the context of mind, a context in which mind or consciousness enquires about itself. Being thus amounted to existence plus reflection. Thus mind became present or meaningful. We were now able to transcend ourselves, that is to say, to gain a meta- or God-position from which to view things. We could leave the prison of the 'I'. At this point being referred to 'me' only as a stage preparatory to entering the realm of 'we', or humanity at large. Subsequently the term has become fractured and thrown into doubt on two levels. Firstly, although it has allowed for matter and minds, it denied that many other things, such as social institutions, are substances. (1) And yet society is currently seen to have a strong claim to be the chief avatar of the human, a claim I will explore in Chapter Seven. Secondly, the Greek attempt to focus attention on humanity at large has given way to a fascination with the subject or the self. Ontology has become a refraction of reality through the viewpoint of the 'I'. Being may still commonly be associated with is-ness. But I will argue that this claim is suspect because of its connection to the 'I.' The idea of being cannot provide an anchor for the human. Only reality can do this.

The concept of being derives from the question: Is a conscious animal a thing or a thought? The Greeks were fascinated by the question of thingness. The theory of the nature of things is a foundation stone of philosophy. Certainly we can say that we humans are in reality and therefore in that sense we are things. But thingness is not all. Philosophy emerges as we see ourselves as more than things: we are also animated. Now we are a thing and a no thing (the immateriality of thought, not to be confused with nothing) at the same time. The philosophical quest addresses no-thingness. But Heidegger took us back to thingness. He was a student of Husserl who tried to anchor humans in subjectivity. Heidegger's Ontological Turn resurrected ontology, but a concomitant epistemological turn (ontology and epistemology being joined at the hip, so to speak) took us to a search for knowledge of being. By letting the thing sneak through the back door of epistemology Heidegger turned the human into a subject or seeker of knowledge of things. Humans are now not just a thing to be contemplated but also an appreciator of reality. But we are not real or a thing in the same way as an animal or stone. They stay true to their nature. We possess imagination and so occupy a separate realm. It is a matter of concern that the enquiry into humanity has been waylaid by philosophy's assumption that humans are bound within the ontology-epistemology relationship. This has stopped philosophy investigating the no-thing realm. Quantum mechanics tells us that when we go deep into things there are no longer things but forces. At the same time, we can take flux or flow to have no shape. But being requires that we hold on to an identity of things in order to handle them intellectually. However identity sets limits on flow. In this case, the idea of being points us to a limit of possibility in humans. But, without a space for possibility, being becomes an imposition.

Drawing on Heraclitus, Heidegger claimed that being arises out of nothingness and that the move from nothingness to being uses the idea of becoming as a stepping stone. However, unless the process is completed, being can never be attained, except maybe in flashes. We will flounder in becoming, somewhere on the journey to completion, rather than achieve a state of being that is able to process what already is. Being does not originate ab initio. The nothing that enables being to be something must be dynamic, a force that impregnates. Conception precedes perception. And we humans are beings before we orient ourselves to the world. Nonetheless an energy generated by perception carries over into being. Socrates told us that unless we use consciousness as a philosophical method it will come back to haunt us. We must first realise that consciousness is not a thing; then we can discipline it and get it to organise our faculties in a way that connects up things. When we use thought as a method we can handle its propensity to turn against itself. We will not be shocked when it starts creating entities and constructs out of the shapelessness of reality.

The development from nothing to becoming and on to something is a cumbrous idea. Somethingness can be seen as a construct we've erected to compensate for our failure to stay with nothingness. So we can relegate somethingness to epistemology. The three-stage model is an attempt to explain the wish of entities to live or to connect. Being lets us down here. We need becoming because being is not sufficient unto itself to reach out to other entities. A better claim can be made for nothingness; indeed it can be seen as a cornucopia of wonders. We can call the notion of somethingness an idol, the worshipping of which obscures God, reality and truth.

The idea of being is elusive. It defies analytic and strict logical thinking. For example, when we fail to be, being doesn't disappear. For an observer it always fails because our mind struggles to engage with reality. Out of this struggle the idea of a conduit between an observer and the observed emerges as a replacement for the failure to be. But, even when becoming fully gives way to being, the encounter with another must be with everything that the other brings with them, and this is difficult to take in wholly. Being is thus a matter of translation, of perception. We can seek to get near enough to comprehend it and distant enough from it to embrace whatever is strange or alien. But 'what is' cannot include 'what is absent,' so what we call being is never all that is present. The signifier-signified duality is an impossible conjunction. It connotes connection and disconnection at the same time; so translation is always also mistranslation. The exercise only works when we leave being in impossibility. If we split being or consciousness into separate spaces nothing is possible because possibility becomes a defined entity. Bergson explains time as the eternal present even though we habitually treat it as space and slice it up. All attempts to define it analytically will fail. The same applies to being. When we recognise this we are not trapped by it.

The notion of being has much to answer for. Nonetheless for a while it found a place in modernism and postmodernism. I've already pointed to traditional ontology's focus on matter and minds, that it denies that social institutions are substances. Heidegger developed an idea that Plato perhaps wisely treated with circumspection. The idea of being tries to tell us about the thing-in-itself, the core of an entity. But when it is made concrete it excludes other beings or cores. Heidegger handled the idea by stripping it down to its physicality (Greek: phusis). This allowed the concept of being to be neither anti-absolute nor anti-metaphysics. It may be that its amenability to conceptualisation is the reason it has held our attention for so long. But being has now virtually disappeared from the canon. Attention has shifted to particularities. When we treat being as the universe construed from a human perspective we realise the same applies to an individual being. This mode of thought carves entities, particulars and things out of wholeness. If we think about ourselves being, thought becomes a property of being. It has not escaped into reality. However if thought is applied to reality, reality wins. Constraints on thought stop us making the latter move. If we are to place humankind in reality we must liberate thought.

One way to explore the realm beyond being is to address the foundational questions of philosophy. Classical philosophy's opening questions are: What is the nature of things? How do we know? And: How do we live a good life? When we reverse the order of questions and put the third (what is a good life?) first, we get closer to an understanding of the human than by asking either what is (reality, things) or how we can know (acquiring knowledge of reality, things). The reason is that the question of how to live a life gives a special resonance to the meaning of witness, observer and perception. These ideas provoke questions about our place in the universe, about purpose, and about how to engage fully with life. They also help us realise that perception runs through all three classical questions. But more than this, we realise that being arises from perception. So, by asking about a good life we put ontology aside. We can now see that humans are merely carriers of mental states and not the states themselves. When we approach a thing we notice its qualities. Being is a quality carried in the thing. A chair is being dressed up as a chair. But does this mean that a human is merely being dressed up as a human? The answer is no when we go beyond thingness. This happens when we let things aspire to be an idea. The capacity to imagine means that humans are not facts but fiction. Philosophy's task is to pivot human imagination from being a producer of social or conventional constructs to becoming an engine of conceptualisation. In this way we will take the human out of the realm of human affairs into the realm of the eternal, the sublime or God.

The way to bring humans to the forefront of thought is to look beyond notions of appearance and being. The idea of human perception (human perception itself, not my own perception) precedes the idea of being. We realise that we perceive before we think about our 'place' in the world. Perception is the universe observing itself. It is a dynamic process that uncovers the appearance of an object. As a perceiver/observer everyone seeks to master the skill of an enquirer. They thereby acquire the properties of a philosopher. But as they look out on the world they might wonder if appearance was there already or, with the Greeks, ask if essence or reality are hidden behind it. Where then is the human 'being'? Since Heidegger, that which lies behind appearance has come to be known as being. So when the universe observes itself (or perception meets being) the human can be said to stand behind it. In an attempt to understand this conjunction we can hypothesise that being is in the realm of appearance and is grounded in human sensibility. Thus, for humans, the purpose of life is to perceive. In contradistinction, the purpose of reality is to be perceived. Plato and Spinoza say the idea of being lies in the idea of perception, and perception places it in reality. However Heidegger put being behind both appearance and us. These ideas suggest that perception underpins enquiry, and that behind both perception and enquiry is the human.

The idea of being has become an attempt to perceive the universe from a human vantage point. But the idea suffers from the fact that consciousness relates or returns to the object on which it focuses. It thus splits that with which it engages from the entity itself. As a result the observer (who would otherwise be an animal or pebble) is disturbed and panics. The bifurcating disposition of the mind has fractured the world into entities, particulars and things. In contrast, reflection arrows back unto itself. It leaves nothing for us to build on.

These moves provoke the questions: Do we discover who we are? Or, do we create ourselves? The latter approach is taken by existentialism. I argue that we do neither because, without consciousness, we would remain an animal. There is nothing to discover, other than to learn or develop practical skills. There is nothing to create. We stay the same. There is nothing to be said about humans because we do not have a nature, or at best we have a half- or quasi-nature. Indeed it can be said that people who are confused (and lack a clear sense of a nature) have more to tell us about being human than those who solidify into successes or celebrities. Successes identify with an activity rather than themselves. They become an avatar of their activity. They cheat by stealing existence from their activity. Famous people recognise there is nothing else left for humanity than to do. More than any other species we suffer a fracture through our core. This is why we have cleaved to being rather than reality. We have lost connection with instinct and instead developed narratives about ourselves. Yet we are indefinable. We have turned to being for something to clutch onto. The only resort that resolves all issues is to apply philosophical method to thought. This makes allowance for the way consciousness has turned us into victims.

Fortunately, the concept of reality can take us where the idea of being cannot. Reality is everything there is. In everyday life people may act as if they are separate from the everything-ness of reality. But the emergence of logos or thought in the Axial Age put humans back into the scheme of things. Logos is conscious there is reality. For this reason Plato was able to treat both being and reality. It can be argued that reality is the only idea that contextualises humankind. Accordingly we can ignore being and argue that there is no core, that things are only anchored in relationship. We can now stop thinking about humans as entities or particulars and free them to move within reality. Quine's nostrum 'No being without identity' categorises people according to sex, age, nationality, and so on. This view treats people as if they are something carved out of reality. No doubt some kind of being will continue to be discerned if people deem it necessary. But my concern is more to do with that which the focus on being has obscured - is-ness. The failure to move beyond being has left us out of touch with reality. Being can be treated as appearance because it arises from a human point of view. But if we see it as a thought it will take us to reality. However, as a thought, a thing will not enjoy a status greater than a non-thing. Even further, the thing can be construed as just as unreal as a non-thing. By staying in the realm of ideas in this way we are able to explore the place of humans in reality. Our search for the human means we must eventually bring is-ness out from under being's shadow.

Philosophy starts with the conviction that humans are not natural. Nonetheless Wittgenstein's claim that philosophy is about the ineffable misses the point. When I look at another human and say I can't ground myself in their nature I am admitting that humans are not what biology, neurology or psychology tells us we are. What these disciplines are speaking about is the non-being of human beings. But this need not lead us to despair about people. At the level of behaviour we can say that all is regression to childhood. The impetuosity and immaturity evident in adults reflects a lack of development. Parents have not assisted their children in the process of growing up. In this sense, humans are developmental projects (cherubim) that 'know not what they do.' They easily lose their minds and regress to the stage of a babbling child.

The early Greek emphasis on reflective thinking may have been unusual even in the Axial Age. Yet our capacity for thinking is what eases us back into reality. Attempts to cut the journey short, such is the notion of being, are best abandoned or at least used advisedly. The current use of the term places being in the realm of appearance because it is seen as arising from a human standpoint. It fails to take us behind all the masks – self, personality, identity, culture, and Freudian defences – to what lies behind, to 'we,' core, process, essence or is-ness. The problem for the notion of being is that we or is-ness resides in the realm of ideas, of absolutes and totalities and not thingness.

We have to accept that our imaginative capacity takes us beyond thingness. We can go beyond the usual meaning of human by trusting things - and trusting humans. In this way we can say that people may betray us, but ideas do not. We fail all the time, but if we dare to think beyond ourselves, the great Axial Age move after all, we can see that we are not failures.

CHAPTER FIVE: THE HUMAN AND THE EXPRESSION OF FEELINGS

'For the body is the source of endless trouble to us by reason of the mere requirement of food; and is liable also to diseases which overtake and impede us in the search after true being: it fills us full of loves, and lusts, and fears, and fancies of all kinds, and endless foolery, and in fact, as men say, takes away from us the power of thinking at all.' Plato, *Phaedo*.

The next claim to be an avatar of the human I will look at is the expression of feelings. As in the case of being, the notion of a self or person retains a tenacious hold. Indeed, a widely-accepted scientific view claims that feelings are both personal and inherent. Developing out of evolution, they arise in the individual brain in response to external stimuli and constitute a component of our 'biological nature.' A more recent contention has it that feelings are constructed. However, whether inherent or constructed, or passed on from one to another, feelings are nonetheless taken to be personal. (1) Indeed current society comes near to according personal feelings the status of prime mover of the human. We need only notice the strength of today's culture of complaint and the rise of identity culture. Stephen Hicks considers that 'the placing of feelings at the root of all value systems' is the crux of postmodernism. 'Rage, power, guilt, lust, and dread constitute the center of the postmodern emotional universe'. (2) Moreover the arts are adept at presenting life as a self-torturing emotional exercise. Matthew

Arnold's poem 'Dover Beach' points to 'the eternal note of sadness' that turned Sophocles' mind to 'the turbid ebb and flow of human misery.'

However classical philosophy views feelings as decoys in the search for existence. Plato assumed we live only at the level of appearances, and this includes feelings. In other words, we haven't even begun to exist yet! Heidegger perceived people to be adept at annihilating existence by projecting their personal issues into the world. The world then disappears, leaving us to handle its nonexistence. Feelings thus seem to serve as a pseudo-existence. Freud broadly agreed, saying that feelings amount only to a representation of reality. They stand at a remove because of what people attach to them - an intensity of experience. When we take experiences to be the mind's interpretation of sense perceptions we cannot be sure how feelings relate to them. Even if we trust a feeling we cannot know to what it refers. Heidegger very nearly bridged the feelings-existence divide by using the notion of dread as a gap through which reality reveals itself. But then he prioritised humans over existence and left the world as a variable dependent on the human vantage point. A strong case can be mounted to say that feelings take us away from reality. However the hypothesis I want to look at takes us beyond questions of the connection of feelings to everything. My point is that our attempts to develop beyond mere existence are obstructed by the way we relate to feelings.

We must return to the first move in philosophy if we are to place feelings in a wider context. Our ability to channel consciousness allows us to become an audience or observer of the world. However this does not mean we are fused with the world we are observing. What we call our experience is only that which our minds make of the world as we observe it. In other words, we are mirrors, reflections or refractions of an autonomous entity - life or reality. This entity is not conditional upon our moods or the content of our minds. Our mind, it must be recalled, is not in reality. And yet the mind succumbs to the addictive power of what it makes of being an observer and is drawn to fuse with the world, thing or other person. Another Platonic insight helps here. What has happened is that we have become attached to our own prism or filter through which we insist the world must pass. This is Plato's Cave, and unless we let in more of the world we will stay in the Cave. The Platonic move is to put all our feelings aside. Instead of saying 'I'm intrigued by the world,' say 'The world intrigues me.' The difference is crucial: I have given way to the world.

Why are we addicted to the world or to the other? One answer is that our inordinate concern for others makes us believe we have irredeemably let them down. I offer this view as the underpinning of the family in the next chapter. The result is guilt or depression. Thus, feelings can be adduced as the basis of a 'human condition.' Erickson tells us that guilt occurs when we fail to negotiate any one of the 8 developmental stages he outlines. But he also says that guilt results from a stifling of initiative. A society that acts against initiatives that threaten its rules and mores is a society of followers. On the other hand, a robust society is one that encourages people to explore what they don't already know. It doesn't wish people to minimise risks, to rely on gaining a glimpse of outcomes beforehand. We could, of course, apply these ideas to love and echo John Lennon's cry 'All you need is love.' Equally we could treat this cry as the voice of an acquiescent society and show courage by reversing it. Reverse psychology would back us up. Betrayal in Christian mythology says that Judas Iscariot turned against Jesus. But, what if Judas is seen as turning towards Jesus and his 'betrayal' proves him to be Jesus' best friend? Judas brought the story of Jesus to its climax. Judas illustrates Plato's contention that animation generates a love of others out of all proportion. The problem is not the absence of love a la Lennon but that we are drowning in love. Instead of believing we let down our nearest and dearest we might now say we don't let them down at all early enough. Judas' lack of remorse parallels that of Meursault in Albert Camus' *The Stranger*. Both were pointing to the misrecognition of love in Lennon's cry. The sooner we stop over-loving the better.

When humans use feelings as indicators of what 'is' they misunderstand the 'is.' Feelings cause self-torment. So, is self-torment a characteristic of humans? Or is our unpreparedness to understand it a more prominent characteristic?

Curiously (because they are thoroughly indulged in literature and the media), feelings are a missing component in current discussions in philosophy and public life. They figure in science as a reaction in the individual brain to external stimuli. These dispositions, it can be suggested, arise because we claim feelings as our own. This possessiveness has the effect of making feelings intense and mystical. We are thrown into a quandary, for feelings are without doubt a connection to reality. They take us fully there. And yet, by making them dramatic, we trivialise them. The strength of feelings frightens us; we defend against this fear by producing an explanation that seems to make them amenable to reason. But this explanation, which we then treat as feelings themselves, merely defends us against the primary feeling. We have mistaken the defence for the feeling. Moreover, this failure to understand feelings, combined with a fear of their extremes, drives us to internalise them. We take it that, by 'consuming' them, we will neutralise their effects. But we end up unsure where we stand. We then act out feelings dramatically because we sense that situations demand certain reactions. But, when we do this, we are inauthentic; we have lost track of the original feelings that connect us to reality. It was this kind of inauthenticity that Meursault in *The Stranger* faced in his local community. In brief, we have yet to learn how to be playful with feelings.

Since the Axial Age humans have enquired about things, given them a name, and engaged or danced with them.

One might think of having a conversation with Death, as in Bergman's film, *The Seventh Seal*. The move to play chess with things, rather than possess them, is the point here. Socrates sought to bring everything into the open space of the Agora or public square and out of the secretive domestic sphere. Things can be discussed there until they are neither a mystery nor a worry. But, when people do not talk, feelings emerge and fill the space. The domestic sphere is the problem. The covering up of thoughts and feelings is structured into domestic life. A failure of conversation only serves to intensify feelings. We see our lives as tragic; accordingly, when someone says 'I feel something,' people salute the remark. But a reference to feelings is an attempt to influence others. A speaker is being rhetorical and using feelings as a connection. And yet he is not asking where they came from or what they represent. The underlying problem of a 'feeling' person is that they see their own lives as the problem instead of looking elsewhere. The problem is their failure to speak. The feeling person grasps onto the signifier (for example, anger) and turns it into an identity. They continue to speak, but internally. This is nothing less than a retreat from life. If the internal fantasy were presented externally it would open itself to truth. But when an internalisation of the world speaks to us as feelings it is neurosis. A therapist treats this as an invitation to convert feelings into speech.

Freud suggests that strong feelings are best left in the realm of appearance. They cover, not a fundamental disturbance of the psyche, but an unfolding of being. We cannot know their ultimate shape. In any case, a wish for a quick definition reflects a fear of indeterminacy. Children can be as intimate and playful as puppies. They quickly rebound from emotional exchanges. We can follow suit: when we treat feelings philosophically we can enjoy what might otherwise be deemed a problem. We can take all to be life, stop thinking of anything as a problem, and instead see it as emergent reality. The probability unfortunately is that our thinking has already been shaped by the culture in which we live. Today for instance, culture tells us our feelings are a problem for which we should take responsibility. And yet, when one says one hurts, it is our internalisation of another's gaze that carries the hurt. It is not ours. All the within is a product of the in-between. Yes, to some extent it may emanate from someone who judges us for being like them. But the pain can best be conceived of as our recognition that the in-between is already processing the 'problem.' There is no need to delimit or sever connection because the in-between is already the boundary between us.

Feelings register what goes on in our lives. Yet indeed, almost anything confers purpose if we make it into an idol. We notice fluctuations in our relation to reality and to past experiences. But this is a very primitive Skinnerian explanation when applied to feelings. It operates at the level of neurological or electrical stimuli/responses of our mind. The real problem emerges when purposes collide.

Then, unless we make everything purposeful, warfare ensues. So purpose in itself is not the issue. But the synchronising of all purposes is a problem, and only truth will do this. Whether people find life purposeful or boring is a psychological matter. Only when it is subjected to persistent thought does it become philosophical.

Feelings ask us to hang in there, for they are playing out a bigger drama that we can presently understand. There is in us something dormant that connects us to reality. It can overcome both appearance in the object and experience in the subject, because both are appearance. Berkeley, Locke and Hume deal with issues arising from the observer-observed syndrome. They help us see that things do not lie in the observer but in the hinterland of our consciousness. I can start out by saying that, as a self, I will live by what I think. I can listen to the words of others, from above, so to speak, from a position or fulcrum beyond myself. Now I realise that people who pull my heartstrings or seem to want to hurt me are not hunting me down or acting at my expense. I can generalise the situation and see that we all take ourselves to be hunted - and yet there is no hunter! Now, by putting myself behind my own gaze and putting people out there as the field of the gaze, I am free of distress. I can continue to seek to know the world. Not to be drawn into the drama of feelings may be seen as heartless. But this is to misunderstand philosophy. When my interest in the world converts the other into an object, the fact that they are also looking at me loses its power to stop me thinking about the world. Thus suffering is eliminated. It is left in the realm of appearance. Nietzsche describes humans as ruminants. They savour things, sit in the sun, and tend to reflect on things only when they go wrong. For them, feelings are the main register of what goes on in life. This makes it difficult for the philosophically-inclined to find others with whom to meet the yardstick of higher truth. Indeed it is difficult to find another with whom to test the farthest reaches of an encounter. This would involve the abandonment of narratives as truth comes within reach.

To be sensitive and empathetic to moods, hidden motives and suffering of those around us is what we usually call soulfulness. But to be empathetic without contextualising empathy can also be a cause of distress in oneself and others. In the spirit that informs this book it can be said that in this case the empathiser is cleaving to an unexamined human viewpoint, not a philosophical one. What is missing is an appreciation of the in-between. This cannot emerge when people are already too connected, maybe even to the point of fusing with each other. Connection presumes two freestanding entities at the outset. When entities are not independent they can become so interconnected that they 'become' the other at the same time as being themselves. We can end up claiming the impossible - to be both ourselves and at the same time to be involved in a nexus of many others (work colleagues, football supporter association, or society at large, for example). We survive only by deceiving ourselves. It may sound harsh, but it is difficult to refute the thought that what is actually happening is that the empathiser has retreated both from life and other people. My point is certainly not that feelings are somehow toxic, quite the opposite, but that we cannot be sure they are our own.

We do well not to ignore the place of feelings in metaphysics. Heraclitus said that nature presents itself in two forms: the material and the immaterial. But, when we treat ideas and feelings as immaterial in the sense that Heraclitus uses it, it is clear that feelings have not gained the attention they deserve. Ideas have gained traction but feelings have been relegated to psychology. This can be taken to reflect the human fear of reality. The Greeks were said to be able to face reality more than other peoples. But in subsequent eras philosophy and society have attempted to appropriate reality in human terms. We can now acknowledge the claim that feelings are real, a claim that is as valid as that of ideas. The 'I' can be seen as the prime culprit. It looks out and gets a brief glimpse of reality and pulls back in horror. Reality is too unformed and untameable to be faced square on. Fear is the result. Our reaching out to fear is a defensive move, but fear itself (as a feeling) is real.

We struggle to know what to do with what is not physical. We fail to accept that something non-physical is not us, that it is another entity. Our thinking has in effect slipped back to the age of mythos that preceded philosophy. The emergence of philosophy (as logos) was so utterly radical because non-material things came to be accepted as just as real as material things. This is fine, but a residual pre-philosophical fearfulness of immateriality drives us to incorporate the non-material into our own mind. By 'swallowing' it in this way we feel safer! The effects of the human urge to domesticate reality are evident all around. We use the planet for our own purposes, domesticate animals, and kill people and other creatures. Yet, as we do these things, we encounter feelings. But then we treat them as our own. We appropriate them to mitigate a perceived threat from the indeterminacy of reality. We can't fathom them. When we try to make them fit into our accepted meanings they end up as an echo of an echo. Yet we have only adopted them. They are not ours to possess.

Moreover we are very capable of detaching feelings from the actions we believe provoked them and releasing them back into reality. This act of appropriation is telling us we can cope with ourselves but not with otherness. The process starts when I encounter feelings but am afraid to address them directly. I say 'I feel depressed' whereas all I've done is encounter feelings. The problem initially rests with language. Our first recourse, as we seek to express feelings, is to the meaning of the words we use, to semantics. There, feelings are usually treated either as a noun or a predicate. In a sentence like 'Columbus discovered America' the discoverer is generally given more importance than that which was discovered. The possessiveness that lies at the heart of subjectivity is built into propositional language. Yet, even at the level of history, America was there before Columbus happened upon it. But there is more to it than this: in a sentence like 'I feel fear' the 'I' is a notional entity and fear is universal. To bring objective reality to the fore in this sentence we need to give the predicate priority over the subject. This move releases reality from human possession and allows us to challenge our fearful response to it. Now the opportunity arises of viewing reality, not with fear, but with wonder. All we need do is leave the feelings as they are and not meddle with them.

Feelings are assumed to be unidirectional, to move from a self towards another entity. But philosophy says: no, feelings are in full pursuit of the world. This is not a matter of one entity reaching out to another, a particular reaching to another particular. In fact the move is in the opposite direction. Feelings emerge to compensate for a lack of relationship between people, or between people and the world. Emergent feelings are complex and little understood. Accordingly people create an inner world of them where feelings start to feed off themselves. This world dissolves into fabrication because imported social thoughts have not received the subtlety of treatment they require. A person then treats the theatre they have created in their mind as a form of personal empowerment or a bulwark against the world. Reality becomes ever more remote.

The idea of the gaze is a case in point. It is associated with the commodification of the object of desire, primarily with regard to women and children but also to the West's attempt to 'orientalise' the East. The true culprit can be said to be the subject-object dichotomy. The transference of early-years experiences into later life and onto others has turned a person into the object of the gaze of others. This is particularly problematic because the gaze penetrates into our deepest innermost secrets. The philosophical move is to turn the gaze around and make the object of a gaze (for example, myself) an outward-directed observer of the world. Now the observer can stand back and start to enquire more generally about things again and stop fixating on particulars.

The philosophical move is always to the meta (the incorporative concept). All mind moves are a pursuit of truth. To release ourselves from the traps of personification and unidirectionality of gaze we must ask how we feel about feeling, not how we feel. This turns us towards reality. The problem here is that the world has traditionally taken goodness to be the measure of all things. We can converse with each other on the basis of goodness about dichotomies such as sadness and happiness. But this keeps the focus in the human realm and invites moral judgements into the arena. Yet, when we make truth the measure of all things, we see its opposite is now falsity and not the other's moral opinions. However humans are condemned to a Janus-faced existence. The reflective capacity of the mind condemns us always to be one move away from what we are. We can fool ourselves that we are addressing reality directly and that this fooling is us. But it is always a second move. Life can seem a perpetual let-down. However philosophy enables us to see reality, not directly or as a burden, but in wonder.

Feelings belong to everyone. Yet they emerge as the IP phenomenon. ('Index patient' is a term denoting the member of a group who is seen as a personal problem in a family, group or society. They are the person in the system who embodies the system. The symptoms of distress that are revealed actually point to hidden patterns in the group's dynamics.) However every symptom is a wish to know. When the wish is not allowed room to express itself it turns into a symptom. When we retreat from life we intensify feelings until they take us over. Melanie Klein says paranoia results when we treat a feeling as a position to be defended. The expression of feelings is often seen by the person concerned as an action because they treat feelings as inner friends. Feelings are thus internal speech. But, where the internal soon becomes fantasy, the externalising of it can lead us to truth. The 'answer' to all issues surrounding feelings is to move towards transcendence. This move does not settle on a point of transcendence (which would amount to a position). But the very movement in that direction opens up thought. We are then forced to ask, not: What is this feeling? but: How do I feel about feeling?

Feelings are best understood as a search for truth. They have risen to prominence under the banner of relativism and in the personal growth movement in postmodern times. 'Don't tell me what you think but what you feel' is a common cry in personal growth groups. But this move risks treating feelings as a personal position or stand. We are exhorted to express them more fully, as if they are somehow freestanding and we can dig into them and find more meaning. But this concretisation of feelings leads the proponent to take up ethic positions and reach for codes of behaviour. Philosophy takes a radically different tack by encouraging all feelings to come into the open where they can offer themselves in the service of the question: What is a human?

So I return to my leitmotif: feelings are an internalisation of the world. They emerge when people refuse to talk. Any move to reality makes it necessary to return feelings back whence they came. An intensification of feelings inside a person denotes a failure to converse. People talk to themselves and then say the feelings are talking to them. The tragedy is that when people commit to feelings as if they constitute their essence they have actually turned against themselves. Feelings arise in the personal sphere where the key energies in life are treated as secrets. This cover-up becomes internally structured and the fantasy treated as reality.

It is obvious that problems become magnified when we give ontological status to the immaterial. In this regard feelings are no different from thoughts. The granting of ontological status might turn out to be even more complex - it can be hazarded that feelings have thoughts at their core and vice versa. We can speculate that feelings are embryonic thoughts. Or we can say that feelings are a move towards thought. It goes without saying that if we are to treat the immaterial the same as the material we must raise feelings from their present diminished status. But we must be wary we don't treat our personal, defensive reactions to the immateriality of feelings as if they are real. So long as we avoid doing this we can return feelings to reality because, when I say I am joyful, I am saying that I partake in joy. I am saying I partake in the universe.

CHAPTER SIX: THE HUMAN AND THE FAMILY

"For many people, in fact, the family is the principal if not exclusive site of collective social experience, cooperative labor arrangements, caring and intimacy. It stands as the foundation of the common but at the same time corrupts it by imposing a series of hierarchies, restrictions, exclusions, and distortions.' Michael Hardt and Antonio Negri, *Empire, Multitude and Commonwealth*.

The family is a popular contender alongside being and feelings to be the core of the human. Freud's 'Oedipal Triangle' of child, mother and father has been seen as offering an abiding explanation of human development. But we must remember that, when Freud focused on childhood sexuality, he was following the zeitgeist which held that unfettered desire causes havoc. Indeed, Oedipus is not an agent in Sophocles' text; the myth is foretold and only enacted later. Oedipus' first move was the killing of his father, which can be read as a symbolic rejection of authority. Sleeping with his mother was only a second move. Indeed, as Deleuze and Guattari point out, the Oedipal idea is first about adult paranoia (the father's fear of losing his exclusive sexual claim on the mother) and only secondly about childhood neurosis. The Oedipal story is best seen as a provocation to ask universal questions. In other words, it is metaphysical.

It asks: Can the family claim ontological status? Socrates would have demurred, saying that the family is in thrall to social and moral values, customs and narratives, to human forces that underpin society. It does not put us in touch with the animation, core or soul that connects us to all things. Each of the parents can be said to be selves anchored in a symbiotic or fused relationship that defines each by reference to the other. Or they can be said to have entered an erotic relationship that overarches the subject-object divide and aspires to a kind of divinity. Both attempts to anchor the couple fail the test posed by the in-between. Both moves look inward for a grounding and not out to the world. Tradition and familiarity strengthen the forces that bind people to each other – the within - and hold at bay the forces of the in-between that turn people' minds to variety, experimentation, adventure and the unknown. Aristotle believed that justice can only hold between individuals who have not fused or become parts of one another. Yet, with regard to the family, Deleuze and Guattari place social investment at its heart: social attitudes are communicated through the unconscious of mother and father. Can we then separate the family from society? Yes, say Deleuze and Guattari. But we can only do this by turning away from what is commonly meant by family (marriage legalities, inheritance of property, parental love-match) and, as a working hypothesis, recognise the child as the essence of the family.

In the most general terms a family comprises a number of people jostling with each other in a kind of un-orchestrated dance. Anthony Giddens follows Engels and adds blood or kinship relations to the mix. But it can be argued that blood and kinship do not colour everyday events and pertain only to tradition and the transfer of property. Indeed the family is not a site of love, hate or other strong feelings any more than anywhere else: these are narratives offered after the event to impose a sense of order (or an explanation) on what is otherwise thinly disguised chaos. The impression that the family amounts to anything more than this derives from the young couple's attempt to burn an inscription into history. They celebrate the creation of something (a love bond underpinned by law that produces an organism capable of reproducing itself) out of nothing. Erotic attraction is understandable in itself, but it amounts to a wish for something outside itself and thereby does not offer a grounding in reality. The notion of family proclaims: We are here; we are undeniable; we stand for virtue and goodness; we are an entity of substance in a world otherwise comprising loosely formed and less well-founded relationships. Furthermore we care for our children and prepare them for entry into a competitive social world, and we safeguard their wellbeing better than the available alternatives. All of these claims come from the mouths of the parents; children are not invited into the executive suite. This is an anachronism, for in recent times adult gender relations have been equalised and adults are free to enter relationships on their own terms rather than on terms determined by tradition or family expectations. This freedom is not extended to children. And yet the family's rock-like quality is affirmed when we say: 'It will always be there for me when others fail me.' The credo, 'blood is thicker than water' is spoken with unshakeable gravitas. Doubtless the family is where consciousness and experience of the world first arise. Furthermore the family offers a unique insight into humanity because the proximity of its members to each other is closer than that usually deemed socially acceptable.

But we can stand these claims on their head. As explained in earlier chapters, somethingness is appearance. The parent's love bond and familial authority rest on erotic impulse, social authority, and inertia. If a family is to be an avatar of humans it needs to throw off the accretions of somethingness and return to nothingness. The first sacrifice would be parental authority. Socrates persistently asks if the family is anything more than a matter of custom and habit that attempts to impose moral and intellectual conformity on its members. For sure in everyday terms the family is a definitional hall-of-mirrors. We accept our origins so readily we deign to question the term we use to describe it. We believe we must belong somewhere if we are to know ourselves; yet, having made the family the site of belonging, we feel imprisoned and struggle to get out. Much distress follows. We can inherently love the one who gave birth to us and yet, if we try to cut the 'ties that bind,' we can end up mercilessly castigating ourselves until our mental health suffers. One thing we can agree about (though it rarely seems to undermine the sanctity bestowed on the notion) is that family is a badly conflicted notion: it comes near to buckling under the weight of its own expectations.

Freud saw it as the place where humanity embodied the contradiction between love and emptiness. Engels depicted the Victorian family as a 'compound of sentimentality and domestic strife.' Is it possible to define the family as an internally harmonious organism that is also at ease with the world at large? Or will these claims be revealed to be superficial or contradictory, even damaging? We must submit them to Socratic scrutiny.

Children are only born biologically, not psychologically. The task of parents is to help the child to be born in all aspects of life. The word 'birth' must be stressed, for parenting is about encouraging the child to explore the unique relation between the new energy it generates and the world at large, and not about being taught how to meet the (past and present) expectations of society. It might be thought that an organism like a family that claims to sustain harmony between its internal parts would recognise that the soul of the child will not emerge in a structure preordained by adults. In a young family, energy and vitality emanate from the offspring: 'The child is innocence and forgetting, a new beginning, a game, a wheel rolling out of itself, a first movement, a sacred yes-saying,' Nietzsche affirms. Its mind and body are undifferentiated. Change is engrained in its thinking. Young children have not yet compromised their integrity by fitting into the family ethos. Furthermore, when Deleuze and Guattari say, 'The child is a metaphysical being,' they are saying the child is of another order to that of the family, that the family is a social imposition on the child. (1) When the child is at the centre, the parents and the Sisyphean task they've given themselves will, beyond the satisfying of mundane daily needs, be treated as a domestic theatrical sideshow for the children's amusement, to which society and the world at large are blithely indifferent.

In this sense, the birth of a child turns its parents into supernumeraries. Evolutionary theory tells us the birth of a child is the death of the parents. The genes have been passed on; there remains no other conclusive function to fulfil. Parents might plead that they know this. Yet, in practice, authority and affection are parental initiatives. When parents worry about their responsibilities regarding the rearing of a seemingly errant child they enhance their own importance even further. Moreover, by seeking to perpetuate romance in their own relationship, they are telling the world that Eros is the node at the heart of the organism and the custodian of values and authority. But the parental love-bond is only a first move which, like a booster rocket, can be jettisoned once take-off has occurred. A love-match is an attempt to bridge a gender divide by letting passion pull two distinct halves together. If the parents try to perpetuate their love match beyond the child's birth the exercise effectively prolongs this thinly disguised arrangement. Indeed, the birth of a child offers the opportunity to abandon the erotic aspect altogether and for the parents to re-join the ranks of a loose-knit assembly of friends. But then passion would have no place, and which married couple will admit this?

When parenthood is a cover for a strong sense of gender difference this fracture will demand constant attention throughout a marriage. This attention can pull the family along in its wake. The job of reconciliation then falls to the child. It is he or she who keeps an eye on the big picture and becomes the philosopher in the family. In the Platonic story a successful search by a human to find its 'other half' allows both to return to paradise. But the child is already paradise. The 'romance of the family' abides in the Platonic realm of appearance.

As a result, the day arrives when the parent's submission to social imperatives begins to haunt the child's life. Children feel compelled to redeem their parents' sins. 'Who has not been the embarrassed guest at family meals where the father or mother treated their grown-up offspring with an incivility which, offered to any other young people, would simply have terminated the acquaintanceship,' CS Lewis asks. (2) The die is cast.

Families exist only in what a child thinks and feels when it observes the hurt in its parents' eyes. We can posit the child being in command all the time and that there is no society and no parents. There is only a child loving an adult. The child works it all out. Set aside all ideological considerations that accrue around the family and we are left with a child making a virtuous sacrifice. It resorts to magical thinking in the belief that, if it hurts badly enough on its parents' behalf, their pain will go away. Children know reality. Childhood is about entropy, exploration, otherness; parenthood is about consolidation, order, hierarchy, trade-off and accommodation. Children and parents face in diametrically opposite directions. The family perpetually ricochets between them. RD Laing pointed to the narrow line we tread between being too much ourselves and thereby falling out of our family and being too acquiescence in the family and retreating into a conflicted mind of our own.

Humans are socialised into being members of an organism. We are not encouraged to see ourselves as wholeness itself. Wouldn't things be different if we treated everyone around us as a child of ours, of us being the parents in other words, instead of us being a child of those who claim authority over us? The general inclination of children is to suffer for those who only give the impression of being strong. Thus, we grow up and become victim-minded; we stay anchored in Plato's Cave. And yet we stay in the cave only because our nearest and dearest are also there and we dare not leave them in agony while we are able to leave.

It must be said that no family fails outright or is necessarily bad. All that can be said is that they have not deconstructed the notion of family. Socrates' key insight into families was that they deny the freedom of the child at their (and society's) peril. For, when parents refuse to look beyond matters of childhood obedience and social training, they produce in their children a resentment and lethargy that breeds a worship of political authoritarianism.

If parents questioned the notion of family they might see that it is the lid of a kind of Pandora's Box where a profusion of forces is dammed up. The chief one (not ills or curses, as in the story) is what the Greeks called agape: a friendship of equals. Whereas erotic love leads the lovers into social bondage, agape leads us into a free association of friends. The Greeks elevated agape to a pantheon occupied by freedom, reality and truth. They recognised agape as a conceptual steppingstone to human fulfilment. The family is capable of becoming a community of friends.

The Greeks were preoccupied with the preparation of young men to be citizens in the polis. The Agora was a vision of rousing public discussions in the public square. It was the final step to the polis. Domestic life wasn't a central issue as such. But Socrates had spotted that the intellectual torpor of the family was a poor preparation for public life. He realised that there is a connection between the hierarchy and authority of the family that easily converts into deference to power in public affairs. Down a long line of causation it produces dictators. Accordingly he located the fulcrum of a philosophical life in the Agora and not the home.

But modernity failed to follow Socrates' lead. Freud focused on the individual; Marx on society; and Foucault on the power of the state. Two of their followers were more attentive to the child. Alfred Adler used his Freudian training to ask about the effect on children of their early interaction in the family. Frederick Engels pointed to the family as a pillar of Marxian economics ('what my departed friend no longer had the time to do.') (3) Michel Foucault identified a series of developments in the eighteenth century that codified the roles of parents and children around the child's maintenance and development. Families were no longer defined chiefly by kinship or social status and became enterprises dedicated to the survival and development of the body of the child. The organisation and regulation of the family tightened up. But Foucault and his student Jacques Donzelot take us no further. Both were chiefly concerned with the way authorities used families as instruments in the maintenance of public order. By insisting 'on family autonomy towards these systems and apparatuses,' (4) Foucault and Donzelot accepted the notion of a unified family and expected it to be protected by the state. At the other extreme, existentialism assumes that humans find it impossible to relate to each other anyway. Its central idea - authenticity - places the self ahead of the other, contrary to the general image of the family that puts the other ahead of the self. Nonetheless existentialism tacitly allows us to fall back upon the notion of the family, albeit one comprising many barely connected parts.

Two claims for the family can be dismissed immediately. Firstly: its reproductive function doesn't mean it operates by the laws of nature. This is a necessary but insufficient condition, for it tells us little about the child as essence. In any case, Leibowitz reminds us that we have had no nature since the Garden of Eden. Nature has no rules governing relating. The gift of consciousness confounds any attempt to explain human action as arising from rules of nature. Secondly, the family is not what people in general (society) say it is. The porousness of the boundary between family and society makes a comparison untenable. An investigation into one serves as an investigation into the other.

Other claims seem more substantial. Firstly: the family is underpinned by love. The star-struck lovers wish to register their bond in the public eye. They buy rings, organise a ceremony and settle on a plot of land. Then love fades and differences surface. By now the couple are a discrete unit set apart from others and sustained by the myth of family romance. Yet there is a danger here that the child acts as a reinforcement of this love. Badiou asks only at this point that the couple 'redeploy' around the child. He is thus able to continue prioritising coupledom as a celebration of love. (5) But Freud discerned in erotic love the beginnings of patriarchy (treated as the worship of authority and not just male power). He viewed adult romantic love as a return to early attachment to parents. Love, in this sense, validates authority. In other words, patriarchy reveals a lack of individuation; it is an attempt to cope with a residual sense of victimhood. The adult victim seeks a rescuer in the other (either or both parents clutching at the child; wife or husband clutching at their spouse). A child who has grown up in this environment lacks the ability to develop adult-to-adult friendships later in life. Adulation of (or vehement opposition to) public figures is a projection of family repressions, a demonstration of a muted state of individuation.

Secondly, families introduce something new into the world. 'Something' here refers to the family, not the child. The idea that something can be created out of nothing has a long philosophical lineage. Heidegger's Ontological Turn was inspired by a Pre-Socratic fascination with the relation of something to nothing. He was more concerned with nothingness, which we might conceive of as flow or flux. In contrast, somethingness is denominating, signifying, particularising, or the drawing of a line in the sand to counter the effervescence, entropy, or even the sheer indeterminacy of the universe. It savours of action, agency and an aversion to flux. Freud's suggestion that all actions are unconsciously provoked supports this view. In other words, action is not agency but reaction. Thus a family that recognised the metaphysical status of the child would cease striving to be something. Nothingness connotes not just indeterminacy but freedom from the pressure of others. It includes what somethingness refuses to acknowledge. To live thus a family must accept the family's dark side. Hatred between members (not just between siblings but of children for the parents and vice versa) would enter discussion, as would resentment against a member who refuses to be stereotyped.

Coupledom would be recognised as a form of emotional rescuing. The sustaining of a realm of somethingness, with its burnishing of particulars, its obsession with appearance and its object-orientation, would end. Chaos could be re-perceived as a source of wonder.

In short, a world of nothingness demands the death of the love bond. Children might be shared among surrogate parents in extended families or communities, a less-structured and more diversified setting that leaves room for satisfaction of developmental needs. Parents can shed their heavy tradition-determined role and adopt sibling-relations with their children. Hierarchies will dissolve; gender rivalries will soften. Breadwinning will no longer confer decision-making status; tight demarcations can be avoided. The family would let things find their place, haphazardly for sure, in a more helter-skelter environment.

The third claim is that a family draws on internal life-forces. In other words, the energy generated within an individual is deemed superior to that generated between people. But the 'within' energy is not self-sustaining: family ethics are imported lock, stock and barrel from society. Everyone struggles with unspoken assumptions about unquestioned rules of engagement. Conversations become a matter of winning arguments or saving face rather than finding common ground. RD Laing's point comes to mind again - we face the horrifying choice of either disappearing into the family or into our own minds. In the latter case an inner world develops, based on monologues and repressed feelings. An apprenticeship in family introversion is poor training for a life oriented to the world. When feelings are expressed within the family they risk being remembered longer than the discussion. Subtlety and con-verse (speaking between, not over or against) are lost. Communication is confined to factual exchange. It has not been exposed to the honest expression of diversity, to the delirium that Deleuze says sweeps away order 'when I seek out my most profound opposite...' (6) Intense, internal differences are smoothed over by compromise.

According to the theory of group dynamics, a malaise in a family (as with any group) has nothing to do with personal failure. We may present one member of the family as needing attention, but it is the dynamic of the family that bears scrutiny. The problem lies in what I've been calling the within. The Greeks told us that energy generated within a person or an entity is appearance. A family that is controlled by roles and rules and doesn't permit movement or dissent occupies the realm of appearance. A fruitful encounter requires two or more open-minded humans to explore issues beyond their personal defences, biases and preferences. They must already have shrugged off the incubus of an inner life of secrets and disappointments. The energy of the in-between is generated only when people are free of narratives and the negative influence of others. In-between energy is essence; it is the source of creativity. It is found as the life of a child evolves amidst a cornucopia of shifting relationships with the world - people, toys and stories. But the family wants the child to abide by the rules of the hearthside.

The final claim is that families are bastions of goodness. The Greeks inherited a belief that goodness stands at the apex of all things where it creates harmony by holding all things together. From the idea of goodness flowed the subsidiary ideas of progress, dependability, and the best ways to preserve wellbeing. When we operate under the aegis of goodness we are able to receive and confer beneficence. Everything on the human level is capable of being enhanced. As it pertains to human wellbeing, goodness becomes akin to the idea of utility; it validates human acumen, will and endeavour. But this validation keeps the family in the realm of self, mind and appearance. The family's association with goodness binds people's thinking to that of others through the medium of common social values (common sense). The attempt of ethics to square contrary human dispositions stops it rising above human sensibilities. These contradictory demands - claiming to harmonise all things familial and societal on the one hand and maintaining a split between good and evil on the other - are not a basis for wholeness. Goodness's claims have come down to us little challenged.

However Socrates brought truth and friendship to the centre of the discussion. Truth doesn't have to reconcile internal differences. It joins up all the dots between us and the universe, revealing binary divides as early moves towards monism. Equally friendship is not fractured by the erotic tensions that arise in coupledom. Truth connects people to the universe; friendship connects people to truth. This means, in short, that the family is an epistemological edifice that acts as a foil against friendship.

This is why Socrates set out to de-familiarise society. He perceived a chain reaction of victimhood spreading from the typical family outwards to society. Young adults would step straight from their social base into citizenship. Yet society is not ready to receive them. It is conflicted: it offers itself both as an absolute that soars above all conflicts and also as enforcer of ethical conformity that destroys the integrity of a citizenry of free individuals. Its association with goodness is never explored. Yet the family clings to the flawed idea of goodness that, Humpty-Dumpty style, fragments wholeness and then strives to glue it together again. Endeavour and acumen are not enough; they are too easily abandoned or misapplied. A universal vantage point is sorely lacking.

Socrates wanted a polis that searched for a congruence of things that only truth confers. Truth offers something goodness lacks. It is universal; it reveals how all things join up. It underpins friendship because it allows people to be independent amidst many competing voices. A fully individuated citizen is free of others' negative influences. Friendship was thus the high road to truth, reality and human freedom. The principle of the Greek syllogism informs the actuality of friendship. It is a model that harmonises relations between multiples by showing how differences seek common ground. In similar bent, friendly disagreement seeks new areas of agreement. Differences are processed by taking the friend's view beyond the point at which the friend has settled. Half-hearted incrementalism gives way to bold hypothesising about universals. Nothing is withheld: contradictions are celebrated. Friendship is free of cloying emotional bonds and obligations and so encourages a swapping of roles. Friendship grants wholehearted acceptance, receipt of straight-from-the-shoulder home truths, equality, the freedom to speak, and the assurance of being heard. It thereby stimulates conversations that go to the heart of things.

Is the family beyond repair? Socialism and the kibbutz movement took it back to the drawing board. But we needn't go that far. All that is needed is that the parent's erotic bond (coupledom) is separated from the family. The family can now be seen as insubstantial. Take away its legal status and nothing is left but the friendship and care it can generate. But this is an advantage, for it now emerges as a group of siblings, of equals. No longer need the adults hide their sense of inner emptiness by taking action that creates unnecessary problems. Emptiness is reality. It doesn't demand redemptive action. In any case, children only need the most general oversight; at most they want companionship. This is where a 'parent' comes in - as a playmate to children, swapping roles and indulging imaginations. The family is now, but only now, the real thing. By centring itself on the essence of a child it transcends self and social bonds and opens its members to reality.

CHAPTER SEVEN: THE HUMAN AND SOCIETY

'In this character as a universal family, civil society has the duty and right, in the face of arbitrariness and contingency on the part of the parents, to supervise and influence the education of children insofar as this has a bearing on their capacity to become members of society...'   Georg Wilhelm Friedrich Hegel, *The Philosophy of Right*.

It bears repeating that Socrates thought that everything that matters in the human sphere occurs when people engage with each other. When they leave behind the custom-ridden realm of the within and enter the dynamic force field of the in-between they channel a potential far exceeding that contained in the self. But not just any gathering deserves the appellation of the in-between. The question boils down to the kind of concourse. Socrates was not persuaded that the life of the polity in Athens asked enough of its members. So he went back to the drawing board. Already convinced that the 'romance of the family' lacks diversity of outlook and fails to question its foundations, Socrates was forced to admit that society was like the family writ large. The idea of a great philosophical gathering in the Agora took shape. A physical public space was already devoted to a mixture of public functions: commerce, a variety of public meetings and philosophical and religious conclaves. But Socrates envisaged a concourse devoted dominantly to rigorous philosophical encounters. A new young man with an opened-up mind would be expected to emerge from the fiery cauldron of the Agora able to devote his new-found freedom in the service of the polis.

What then were the deficiencies of society for which the Agora would compensate? The Greeks were convinced that we are constructed socially. But, beyond a certain point, society's appeal to loyalty imprisons thought. It has come to underpin humanity by default. Socrates was convinced the notion was not fully worked through. In our time, social theorist Bruno Latour conceives of society, not as a transcendental single whole, but as potentially endless assemblies in the process of construction. He doubts that the social constitutes a special domain. Yuval Noah Harari gives a nod in this direction when he defines society as little more than its own narrative. Freud would have called society a place where a multitude of personal defences gang up against a fear of infinity or indeterminacy. Sociology tells us that society splits into ever more identity groups the more it develops. In an attempt to maintain a false equanimity, Foucault points out, society hides the 'problems' of criminality, madness and sexuality. Indeed Deleuze tells us things will never cohere and that essence is irrationality itself. Indeed, when we stop viewing humanity through rose-tinted glasses, it can be argued that an authentic conversation between any two people is impossible. (1) Society can be viewed as nothing but a collection of selves augmented by the power of imagination. Not only is there no in-between but there is the barest vestige of a within! In response to this dilemma the Greeks exhorted us to go beyond our own position and become inspired by another person. This exhortation takes us to the heart of otherness, and otherness leads us back to Greek idea of wholeness. However otherness involves an acceptance of that awkward, contrary person we usually try to avoid. This person's contrariness will prick our bubble of isolation and challenge our penchant for surface talk only too easily. As a result, it is difficult to accept talk of the cohesion or totality of society as anything but an illusion. Indeed, when the human is split at its core, as I have argued from the outset, it behoves us to turn our attention away from society's cracks. Society doesn't come near to coping with what is wrong at the heart of things – humanity – because society stands opposed to indeterminacy, flux and chaos.

Society has an almost mystical power to project itself as an anchor for humans in the world, equal only to the self. So, as an opening gambit, we can treat the notion of self as constitutive of society. Selves can be called the separate parts of the whole. Yet we immediately run into a problem. Freud tells us that relationship precedes the self. The self is a defence that is built when a child faces the pressures of the adult world. So it follows that relationships between people precede society. Nonetheless, the self has in effect swallowed up or internalised relationships with others in postmodern times. That is to say, the in-between has disappeared into the within. Our selves have been turned into monstrous edifices that attempt to contain whole worlds of interaction that would otherwise be played out in the public arena. Society tells us to protect other selves by sublimating or battening down our own feelings in case they overflow and cause social havoc. Yet a relationship is already a boundary between self and society. When it is left to itself it can carry all before it. Neither self nor society needs protecting. Yet selves clearly struggle. They seek support to carry their overload of identity by joining groups in defence of legal rights, personal feelings and social sensitivities. Yet humans are already interactive; they do not need to be marshalled or to seek solidarity. Public discourse that sets selves against society is disingenuous or manipulative: there can be no society (as it presently stands) without selves (as they are presently understood). Yet more telling is a rarely-mentioned dichotomy: the notions of both self and society stand in opposition to the intrinsic human urge to relate. The pull of humans to each other has been obscured by the loud voices of self and society. Social role-playing has replaced human engagement. When we think we have found someone unique we are likely to be shocked to hear the same formulaic social points tripping off their tongue.

Society is an intellectual construct awaiting philosophical deconstruction. It has been described as the narrative to which people collectively subscribe, a network of self-interpreting individuals, the sum of all human differences, feelings and behaviours, or an attempt to organise people in the aggregate. Yet, rather than returning us to the flux and entropy of reality, it can be described as appearance meeting appearance. Indeed it is not a huge step to describe society as an extension of family dynamics. Aristotle deemed it necessary for a polis to comprise different types of men; only then would people offer variety instead of uniformity to each other. Cooperation doesn't involve each doing the same but each contributing what they excel in. Indeed, it is not frivolous to say that society is the sum of teenage attitudes. The 'teens are years when children seek to reassess their place in the family nest and to reorder their lives. This involves holding a precarious balance between adventurous engagement with the world and personal consolidation. Similarly society lurches back and forth as it broadly tries to sustain some sort of equilibrium.

Indeed, the idea of society assumes that people have already been suborned into conforming to norms. As such it offers only a simulacrum of friendship. In this case we can be said never to have related in our lives. We live through, not in, relationships with others. We pick up a vision, meaning or purpose in another and make an idol of them. The closest similarity is to an artist who creates very interactive people and relationships in his production that are almost certainly more real than those in his own life. It's there in the story of Pygmalion; we glimpse it in Passoa's lines: 'I'm the character of an unwritten novel, wafting in the air, dispersed without ever having been, among the dreams of someone who did not know how to complete me.' More mundanely, clients in the caring professions can be 'loved' as if they are real friends, despite the brevity or role-limited form of association. But these are simulacra, imaginary. A life lacking self-appreciation drives us to sustain ourselves by reaching out to made-up versions of others' lives (literary, imaginative or otherwise). This is the context that produces life-as-a-narrative, life that has been constructed from imported meanings and forms.

In matters social, things have tipped decisively in one direction in the modern and postmodern eras: personal experience is now treated as the measure of all things. For example society validates falling in love and laments falling out of love. Yet, we all know how easy it is to become enamoured of another and, with Pushkin, we can recognise that 'Unrequited love is not an affront to man but raises him.' Further, society's commitment to dichotomous (win-lose) thinking and to setting one political creed or interest group above another leads to a fight to the death, to a desire to have the last word whatever the outcome. These are dangerous signs. Society is capable of acting against itself and creating the very anti-social currents it sets out to avoid. What is clear is that the notion lacks philosophical scrutiny. It needs to stand on sounder foundations if it is to withstand attack.

Why then do we cling to social values when they keep us from truth? Psychology tells us this occurs because socialisation is a passive process. Needy children do not question what they are offered in the family or school. They unquestioningly adopt their parents' attitudes, which tend in any case to be socially-derived. If a child is to individuate the parents must encourage them to question, instead of transmitting, social values. The child must find within itself the courage to stand apart from the ruck. Otherwise we will become recipients of all the negative influences and pressures transmitted by the people around us. This nexus is what I mean by society: it precedes the idea of humanity. Passoa says that humans are victims of their ability to become part of that to which they feel kinship. The problem is not that this occurs, but that we do not include this move in the search for truth. Instead, we disappear into the thing with which we feel kinship as if it is part of the very essence of our self.

Psychology tells us that we become beings by gaining recognition from others and that our craving for interpersonal recognition (friends and loved ones) never goes away. But society offers itself as a powerful recognition-conferring source and from early on starts to superimpose itself on the interpersonal zone. Social recognition offers a status that individuals can chose to set above that provided by their friends. A socially-recognised role (soldier, law-enforcer, graduate, professional, carer) and a rank and place in society come attached to society's conferment of recognition. Friends do not provide this. But why would anyone prioritise functional or status-laden recognition over that provided by warm-hearted, supportive friends? The first form of recognition is remote and it asks people to conform to rules that would disabuse an accepting friendship.

Yet I suggest that this is how we relate to the idea of society. We emerged from the Garden of Eden without anything substantial to fall back on and have had to live with this Big-Bang effect ever since. Without a fixed nature we are capable of anything: we create and recreate, relate and dissociate, are loyal and betray, we nurse things and abuse and kill them. It seems that the endless possibilities of our situation are a bigger curse than the limitations upon them. We abandon our imaginative faculties as we enter the social zone. Possession of an imagination means we can think of any scenario or eventuality. Our minds will create secret friends and alternative families hiding at the bottom of the garden. We no longer need our declared friends. This is scary for them; it reminds them they are dispensable. Moreover it becomes clear that imagining things is better than doing them. Doing confines things in the realm of experience; imagining does not. But society is suspicious of imagination which doesn't seem to offer the full Monty; it stops us getting up close and personal with an actual other. And so, on behalf of others, we abandon imagination and stick to practical actions that can be administered. We are free but have not faced up to it. Puzzled and easily panicked, we compromise. Our default position is to be neither something or nothing. Possibly because we fear anarchy will result ('keep a hold of Nurse for Fear of finding something worse') we don't allow ourselves to ask questions outside the box of social verities. We end up as a retreat from what we could be (or are).

Society is not all: people have pursued human connection in many forms other than the social. We need only think of interpersonal relations such as love and friendship. Society is merely the tip of the iceberg of human connection. Socrates and Plato took the Greek Agora or public meeting place as their starting point. The self was to be left at home because the participants in the Agora understood that all issues are to be philosophised. Discussions would exclude psychological, political or media-driven attempts to seek knowledge or solve problems. We can surmise that these two great minds hammered out the hypotheses discussed here.

Social narratives seem capable of resisting every challenge. We are told we are born into society and that it follows us to the grave; that it can do without us but we can't do without it. Hegel rationalises it and gives it intellectual validity. He treats society as a particular part of the whole of reality. But it is our job here to set it against the backdrop of the absolute. We can start by pinpointing some suppositions in the construct. Firstly, Hegel's comparison of the individual and society is a mistake. Both are cases of appearance. Indeed the assumption that they are comparable might be a cause of the neurosis that results when we vacillate between self and society. Secondly, society is associational; it requires one only to abide by the rules of authority to be brought within its ambit. Thirdly, people are connected by more than aggregations such as solidarity or socialism. The latter tell us we are equal, but equality may not be enough to bring us together. A philosophical approach requires that we go all the way to totality and not stop at any single idea on the way. People turn to other people for succour, to people who inspire them, to those they wish to emulate, before they reach out for social recognition or support. This is the crucial move. Until we deconstruct the notion of society it must remain a collective delusion, a front for something more real. This is not to say we should wish it away; rather, that we should recognise that it needs philosophising.

Society is an 'overdoing.' We feel driven to help others too much. The moral status of responsibility and blame is cast in stone. Certainly, the longing for connection that consciousness has conferred on us is universal. All the same, it is not ours personally. Blame and responsibility are attempts to restrain our longing - and yet our longing is the result of being conscious! How crazier can blame be? Indeed, action (in response to a feeling of being blameworthy) without thought is dangerous. Socrates told us we should first remove the blockages in our own perception. What seems to require us to be or do good, on further examination, reveals itself as a chimera. We easily overreact and pay a high price for it. The world is fine anyway. It doesn't need attention beyond the fixing of mundane tasks. All problems that are seen as major are only so because we have picked them out from myriad others. All that is needed to resolve most things is a disposition, a skill, or encouragement; The simple advice: 'when you have dug yourself into a hole, stop digging' would carry us far. It is there in the Greek term meden agan (Nothing to excess) inscribed on the temple of Apollo at Delphi. It is there in the Greek term hubris (insolence or excess). Ironically problems arise in the urge to offer solutions.

Thus we can treat attempts to improve society as missing a crucial point. They focus on content and not process, on administrative efficiency and not underlying reality. This urge to improve practical mechanisms diverts us from the task of questioning the idea itself. The drive to improve things is magnanimous; it reveals a nobility of spirit. But philosophy is a corrective move. It sees the mind that is applied to administrative efficiency (and not administrative efficiency itself) as fallen. There is no reason for governments or people to be ashamed or to see themselves as failing, and thereby to respond by trying harder or looking for a scapegoat. It is just that the mind operates in contradictory ways. The superego and its concomitant bad faith arise from the mind and bear down on people, causing a diminution of self-love. The result is a complaining, confessional or retributive society. We commonly respond to perceived problems by fixating on a supreme idea. In this case it might be efficiency, need, wellbeing, or resource allocation, all of which push the original, more general question of society itself further down the road. Philosophy asks us to enquire into the underlying idea and not into particular issues, administrative niceties or even the character of those charged with implementing them. The search is for truth, not improvement or blame. In this way the idea becomes a fulcrum that underpins our search for richer possibilities. We find we can do more for human wellbeing by pondering the idea of society than by constantly tinkering with social mechanisms.

We can heed Plato and take society back to source. Only then will we deduce in this process a person as yet unmade and ready to spring forth. This person will have a receptive and accessible mind that, by being well-anchored, can open to others. This has yet to happen. Truth is the only guide in our search. And the road to truth does not emerge from the individual human mind. It emerges from the process that informs conversations between friends. These conversations can resist society's curbs and let imagination run riot. It must be remembered that, in the absence of imaginative outbursts, we would not have the finest symphonies, novels and plays. The work of Einstein and other great minds arose from acts of imagination. But there is no need to act out all our imaginative gambolling: instead of acting out paranoia we can discuss it. The symbiosis of self and society has at best allowed humans to sublimate their wildest dreams. We can return to what the Greeks denoted as the in-between and Julian Jaynes calls the bi-cameral mind. These ideas convey a sense of the staggering power of encounters in the Agora. Psychosis has no agenda or dogma. In Deleuze's terms it operates in the fashion of a rhizome. It is generated in the unconscious where it allows thoughts to spread everywhere under cover. It makes unexpected connections and follows unpredictable angles of flight.

Society's penchant to separate the goodies from the baddies points to the binary thinking that lies at its heart. Society reaches out to ethics because it desires to accommodate most people. They and it are being asked to restrain themselves or be accused of hubris. Even the libertine Greek gods condemned Prometheus to a living hell for passing fire to humans. Icarus was warned not to fly too high. In the Bible Joseph was condemned to be devoured by beasts because he was boastful. But imagination sits in the opposite corner to binary thinking. It is not surprising that society struggles to handle it. Polar opposites are embedded at the heart of current public discourse. We can think of an Oxford Union debate, a typically cautious ('both sides of the argument') newspaper article on a contentious matter, or the oppositional format of criminal courts. And yet it need not be this way. An encounter is the meeting of two points of view, two 'rights' so to speak within a relationship, not between a right and a wrong. In the latter case wrongness has been inserted deliberately in order to create a dichotomy. This move fails to recognise that dichotomies are always false. They hide something bigger. Lying behind the binary divide is a connection. Dichotomies are way-markers to bigger things, to a deeper realisation of the potential in an encounter.

In any case, a move towards reality has already been made in the form of our longing. A second move is unnecessary because the world will respond to the first. To assume it is our task to respond is to interject the human into the reality of things. We need do nothing. This will give reality room to move. Certainly we know that longing produces movement which in turn generates a counter-movement. We can take it that others struggle with this tug-of-war. So we can actively undo exaggerated versions of the drive to do good by including the other in our own move away from responsibility. The world or reality is all. Indeed we could ask: How on earth can one claim to speak for it? Only now can the search for intimacy take its course.

A philosophical approach pitches the notion of society against metaphysical ideas such as origin, source, wholeness or connectivity. We need to know what pulls people together before we ask how they function when together. Society is more than a network or functioning aggregation of individuals. Indeed human connection preceded society. Individuals seek more than association, identity, security, or utility. People are receptive, accessible and porous. Their very openness and affectivity means they cannot be treated as isolated units. The space or connectivity that lies between them (the in-between or, a more recent term, the interpersonal) must be our starting point. We want answers to the questions: Where does society fit in the great scheme of things? Has it primordial origins or metaphysical possibilities? Or is it only a provider of security, services and identity?

We can start with human connection. This tells us that a person is nothing else but a tilting towards the interpersonal. The notion of a freestanding individual now disappears. By turning attention from the particular to the absolute we can see that the cracks in the practises of society are nothing less than life unfolding, and not signs of failure. The cracks are reality itself. The interpretations woven around the cracks are narratives, but the cracks that the narratives attempt to explain are not. The focus now shifts from matters of morality and utility to a search for truth.

What pulls us to each other (love by another name) is a mystery. It may comprise the dark energy of physics that moves the universe, for all we know. The problem lies between people, not inside them. As an enquiry into society, philosophy focuses on concepts like otherness, the interpersonal and the conversation and not on the happiness or psychology of the individual. This is because the emergence of consciousness has created an unremitting longing for engagement with reality. Consciousness flows through a person in search of the reality of another. Yet, as a longing for connection grows, it produces a countervailing revulsion against the other. The impetus that drives people outwards beyond themselves makes them want to explore the totality of the other and satisfy an intense desire for intimacy. As we enquire deeper into the other more things emerge; but we are not satisfied with this and push on too far. Total connection with or absolute knowledge of the other is deemed impossible and despair sets in. Thus intimacy reveals extreme differences between people to be horrifying. So, when consciousness and reality clash, we feel trapped, both attracted to difference and wanting to distance ourselves from it. We fear an embrace of the other will annihilate our self. And yet, if we hold on to a sense of self, we fear we might trap all of reality in our mind. Out of this dilemma emerges society. It sits at the tipping point between the individual and the other, the object, or reality. Society operates by the conviction that it is impossible to move either forwards or backwards. But unfortunately it fails to conceptualise this impossibility. Heedlessly running with this thought it doesn't notice that it has forced thought into either/or choices. Thoughts are now never just thoughts but are about judging whether something is good or bad. Some judgements are deemed more acceptable than others. For example, society's cautious, unphilosophical disposition makes it lean (on balance) against intimacy. The cause of social failure is human failure and society cannot handle it.

Durkheim found human divinity in human congregation. It can be added that the opposite is also true: that groups fail to deliver what they ostensibly promise. Accordingly society is Janus-faced: it promises completion while always failing to deliver to the promised level. The same can of course be said about any form of human connection, friendship and love for instance. This happens (and here I invoke Plato) because a group is an idea. It is full of possibilities that may not be actualised.

There is no guarantee that the idea can be converted into practice. On the other hand, it may be that the very move to actualise the idea provides enough impetus for less-well-developed friendships or partnerships to be sustained under the umbrella of the idea. An attempt to live out an idea might be sufficient to keep open the possibilities of the idea. It can be said that groups never become more than an idea, but that nonetheless they enable being to occur. This might apply to society. It certainly seems to have applied to the Greek Agora, which stands as an example to us today.

A precondition of a wholehearted encounter is that the self and personal narratives are left at the door. Only then can a process be elicited that would otherwise lie dormant within the encounter. Society shuns this realisation. And, having insisted that encounters are the meeting of opposites, society has to ameliorate or soften the arbitrariness or harshness of its judgements by drawing on credos like 'crime of passion,' 'extenuating circumstances' or 'diminished responsibility.' In philosophical terms we can say that an organisational body like society struggles to cope when consciousness is applied to it. A field of interaction opens up that risks spiralling out of control. Nonetheless, as a working proposition, we can say that the wellbeing of society depends on an understanding of consciousness. Is society able or prepared to go there?

Society cannot produce a free citizenry, Socrates' dream. As presently understood, it cannot felicitously handle the assembly of people. Of course, when philosophy releases movement by focusing on consciousness's enquiry into reality, it is aware that this is also being played out at the human level. It conceives that human longing for others will attract a response from the world at large. But when humans intervene pre-emptively they short-circuit the world's response. In order to allow things to keep moving, philosophy has to focus on movement for its own sake and to ignore human intention or outcome. Humans are not responsible for the generation of universal forces. Nonetheless the ancients considered the pre-emptive intervention of humans into the world's affairs to be the cause of human ills. Society is the outcome of this intervention. Of course Plato's views on polity can be criticised. But we must thank him for putting society under the spotlight. It still remains little understood. So, until it has received more penetrating philosophical critique, we must hold the notion in suspension.

In the next chapter I ask a question that fascinated Plato: Why do humans treat appearances as real and ideas as unreal?

'Since every assemblage is collective, is itself a collective, it is indeed true that every desire is the affair of the people, or an affair of the masses, a molecular affair.' Gilles Deleuze, *Dialogues II*.

The socio is an illusion that convinces us that humans can connect to each other; it prevails only by common consent. My general argument has been that we are alone, and can't even connect to ourselves! Yet the socio fights against this realisation. Were we to run with the idea that we connect in any sense at all, it would be to everything. We would then be able to admit we do not know anyone as a particularity. But the socio reacts against this realisation because it operates by holding everything still, as in a snapshot. But differences occur only when things are immobile; when they move there is no difference. When things are allowed to flow problems go away. Why then has the socio created a problem it then offers to solve? It responses to the human failure to individuate, to detach from early carers. When we individuate we realise that lack of connection does not take away joy, for only then are we able to open our eyes to the full glory of the human in front of us. They are full of subtle differences beyond our ken. We am encountering a mysterious person whose every aspect intrigues us. Life is full of wonder.

But a desire to particularise and then possess the other - to fix reality in our favour - won't go away. The Greeks believed that, ultimately, philosophy will relieve the distress caused by this desire. It will correct the infelicity with which we use the gift of consciousness. But, in the absence of philosophy, a grand human edifice like society fails in its primary task of relating individuals to each other and to the mass of people. The result is that individuals in the same moment feel alone in a crowd and fear losing themselves in others. Socrates' vision of the Agora offered to resolve this issue by producing fully-individuated citizens for whom contact with others was free of possessive desires and its concomitant, dread of fusion. Social intercourse would become a form of intellectual exploration which shunned opinion-bartering. No longer would personal thoughts and feelings be considered real and ideas be dismissed as unreal. The Greeks were able to place personal autonomy on a pedestal because they understood that it is impossible to face others or to philosophise without it. No one else now controls one's thoughts. The Greeks rejected the power of a king or Pharoah to symbolise the unity of their community. Independent citizens wanted to thrash things out exhaustively among themselves, to take as long it required, and not to have a quick answer imposed on them from above. As Pericles said, '...instead of looking at discussion as a stumbling block in the way of action, [we Athenians] think it an indispensable preliminary to any wise action.' (1)

Today we lack an Agora spirit: the within, expressed through self, family or society, has subverted the in-between. Appeals to similarity carry a potency that is said to be lacking among autonomous individuals who gather to hammer out momentous issues. Yet the result is that people anxiously question their actions, thoughts, feelings and relationships - and this is accepted as normal. The emergence of the other disrupts the search for personal wholeness and begs the question whether the parts of a whole can be integrated. We are split down the middle. We try to be ourselves and be with others. This is difficult to resolve. The struggles of the human may be said to be their beauty – and the beauty of society that sits uncomfortably atop this struggle. But this means we have settled for greeting others with a wary bonhomie, not in wonder at the magnificence of the differences they bring to us. Society is an aggregation of capricious, non-autonomous and over-defined selves borne down with ethical judgements and political opinions. How can we accept a society that so little understands its task?

One reason is that society's very beginning was strewn with problems. From the outset, it failed to address a dilemma at the heart of humanity. The emergence of consciousness has thrust a wedge into the fabric of the universe. The result is an illusion of dualism. Humans are left with an invidious choice. One option is to internalise this split as an individual experience. But this has led to the appearance of an ethico-epistemological hybrid. A Hobbesian belief that humans are vulnerable to each other has produced the edifice of ethics, a search for knowledge in order to clinch arguments. The second option depicts people as members of warring factions. This option accounts for political philosophy. Both philosophical constructs indicate a failure to integrate being and consciousness into an all-encompassing oneness. This failure has left space for a simulacrum of oneness to be offered by a powerful force. This is what I mean by the 'socio.'

Plato turned the illusion of duality into an opportunity: he hypothesised that a battle of ideas rages behind our perception of the world. But these ideas are still-born. The energy of the within holds sway. The problem is that only fully individuated people can access the energy of the in-between. In other words, one needs to be free of the influence of others if one is to think conceptually. Drawing energy from the in-between, conversationalists are able to follow imaginative and conceptual flights of fancy and introduce fluidity and the unexpected into human affairs. But when people lack autonomy they seek to pin things down and throttle every burgeoning thought at birth. The failure to implement the idea of the Agora not only keeps hidden an all-encompassing oneness, it seems to have widened the gap between the apparent world and its underlying ideas beyond reach. The result is that people can't make a clean contact with each other. Doubting that relationships will hold, people sink under an oppressive self-regard. Life becomes insufferable. The socio is an attempt to do the impossible – to connect people together. It denies the power of individuation to make a clean contact between humans.

The term 'socio' derives from the Latin for interactions or bonds between friendly people: socius. Gilles Deleuze and Felix Guattari adopted the latter term in *Anti-Oedipus* to refer to the social body that takes credit for production of desire and to its encoding by capitalism. My focus however is on the ideas that human assembly attempts to shape. The socio has been the underlying theme of Part Two. I will for the present call it a force that emerges when our thinking solidifies into opinions and value-judgements. Feelings, family or society are construed by reference to this force. It answers a call for protection against the instability and unfairness associated with reality. However the worship of opinion entrenches a set of ethical and political norms that dominate human affairs.

The socio lies in a niche traditionally occupied by the soul in classical philosophy, the Spirit in Hegel, power in Foucault and the id in Freud. In order to create a space for fresh thought we can put aside other contenders like the All, God, mind, Spirit or zeitgeist, history or will. In brief, the question of the socio forces us to hypothesise that beyond many layers of accepted thought, zeitgeist and particularity lies an 'elemental' thing to which all can be reduced. It originates in a proclivity of humans to draw together. Yeshayahu Leibowitz observed the capability of people to ignore wide differences of background in order to devote their lives to a common cause. Yet, hypothesise as we may about the elemental nature of this underlying force or about worlds beyond the senses, we must nonetheless admit that we live our lives in the apparent world. It can be the cause of nightmares when we realise that behind us lies a world that itself hides an elemental universe. How many more realms are there to discover? What indeed lies behind our consciousness and will?

The Greeks contended that actual things derive from an idea. They raised questions over society as we know it: the 'actuality' of institutions, rules and mores. We must step back a moment to conceive of the Axial revolution. It drew inspiration from an understanding of the awkward early years of our lives. When a child realises his parent(s) are no longer prepared to wait on him hand and foot he will react against this perceived neglect by constructing an identity or self. This secures him a safe place among his fellows (and alongside his parents). The result is that, by the time he is an adult, his identity is an amalgam of many opinions and values. Society's task is to mediate these opinions; yet, given that they themselves are socially-generated, the task merely serves to entrench inertia. Socrates wanted opinions to be brought into plain view and pitched resoundingly against each other. They were expected to collapse under the glare of scrutiny or be exposed as the sum total of human defensiveness. Now conversation would nurture souls; the space that lay outside the self, experience and opinion would be explored. Ground was cleared for a society that was exposed to reality.

However the socio has survived because we treat it as totality, All or reality. It stands in the place of God. This move has allowed the mental edifices such as family and society, to develop lives of their own. They've become institutions with the power to prevent individuation. Moreover they muddy the water regarding Platonic monism, which says that everything in life is appearance or content until it is deconstructed. Now everything in life operates under the aegis of the socio. But its deconstruction is rebuffed by appeals to the sacredness of human sensibilities, themselves deriving from an assumption that an irreducible core lies at the heart of socio-generated society. In other words, society is deemed to be more ontological than reality.

When people do not individuate they accept society as a spectacle, a happening, a bid to look solid. They do not question its detachment from the flux of reality. It has become a thing. But classical thinking understood reality as nothingness or indeterminacy. Only that which didn't happen, or might otherwise have happened, is real. Thus a happening, a something, must be collapsed back into what is not known or apparent, from whence it came, for it to become real. Failing this move, a happening or spectacle remains a human construct, a simulacrum of reality. The Greeks were familiar with the way spectacles can induce catharsis. But catharsis is only a partial escape from the anxiety generated by a life closed to reality. Society keeps reality at bay and yet it still doesn't offer relief from the distress caused by this move. People are beholden to society both to satisfy their wish to escape reality and for relief from the anxiety caused by the desire to escape. Bright and shiny on the surface and lacking ontological foundations, the social structure erected on the foundation of the socio induces in people a wish for the impossible. Firstly, we wish to know ourselves in order to mitigate the isolation of selfhood. Secondly, the search for connection is a wish to belong. Neither wish can be satisfied. Depression and a sense of victimhood are the result. People ignore Nietzsche's attack on the god Apollo, above whose temple was inscribed the motto: Know Thyself. Freud drove Nietzsche's message home: We cannot know ourselves. In contradistinction, Socrates envisaged citizens being able to turn outwards to reality because they realised there is no need to fear indeterminacy. There is thus no need for a self. He aimed to sweep the Aegean stables clean with a blast of reality. He encouraged humanity to face the entropic tendency of reality, to give up trying to turn self and society into islands of order in a sea of entropy. He was saying that individuals achieve autonomy only when they can handle a fear of indeterminacy.

This is not just an issue of aggregation, of the forces released when people come together. I make a Platonic assumption that the idea of the socio (as with any idea) is much bigger than we presently think it is and that it is presently acting as a cover for other ideas that can potentially subvert it. This idea is telling us in the most emphatic terms that the relegation of reality has made the thinking and behaviour of an individual human a variable dependent on the perceived thinking of the mass of humanity. Solipsism reigns; conformity is entrenched. Vitality is drained out of thought and replaced by narratives. The socio is an idea that explains the matrix. But the reach of the matrix cannot be total, otherwise the very exercise I'm involved in here would be foretold. A smidgeon of reality has to be left as a window into the system. This is done by assuming that socialisation is never complete, that something in individuals escapes total conformity. As complex and contrary as we may be and as able as we are to hold opposing views simultaneously, we are never fully autonomous. This is the price we pay for obsessing over others' opinions, for fusing with the mass. To a greater or lesser extent, and mostly greater, we as individuals are possessed by an external force.

The result is that, even though the self ostensibly sits at the centre of things, we perceive ourselves as diminished, as smaller than we are. Heidegger claims that reality lies in front of us and 'unconceals' when we look at it. What if there is something behind us that is concealed? Freud said that, whereas Copernicus showed that humans are not the centre of the universe and Darwin revealed humanity to be just another chain, he showed that we do not know what is in our own minds. This diminution starts in Plato. He originally treated the mind as the force that moves all things. However, by the time he wrote the

Republic he no longer shared Socrates' trust that people are reflective enough to individuate fully. He doubted that people in general will use their minds philosophically. Accordingly, he drafted a top-down system of governance for an ideal society. Freud's idea of the unconscious moves in tandem with Plato's *Republic*. The unconscious is a repository of all that a person fears to reveal to the world. Plato and Freud suggest that a generalised repression of animation arises from a dread of unfettered connection. The only choice offered by our fearful reaction to animation is to choose between channelling or personalising this dread. A conviction that we might be bigger than our thinking indicates has long since disappeared.

The socio's claim to totality raises questions about the origin of things. The search for an idea that can encompass all differences preoccupied the Axial Age. Deleuze and Guattari are able to place multiplicity at the root of all things because: '...the Pre-Socratics had already grasped the essential point for a determination of science, valid right up to our own time, when they made physics a theory of mixtures and their different types.' (2) We can apply this idea to the aggregation of humans, to society itself. A gestalt insight tells us that, when entities aggregate, the sum is greater than the parts. Put another way, relationship precedes the individual. For example, when we emerge into the world we find others (mother, couple, family, carer) already there. Indeed, the idea of the a priori tells us that plenitude lies at the heart of nature. Nature is over-abundant to the point of wastefulness: a large majority of seeds die before a few go forth and multiply. We survive individually because of the prolificacy of the mass that preceded us.

The Greeks expressed this idea in terms of the love that entities show for each other. The very defining of an entity rips a part away from the whole. Plato used the imagery of a lover in pursuit of a beloved to illustrate the move of the part back to the whole. Return to origin is expressed initially as the impulse to conjoin with another. Indeed, we would not be extending Plato too far to say that being would not be available to humans without love. Being doesn't manifest, whereas we take it that love does. Plato's idea of love proffers it as integral to a process of return; but this process has already incorporated us. We don't love; we *are* love. In which case, once we are integral to a process, we partake in all aspects of it. We have returned to the idea that the sum is greater than the parts and relationship precedes the individual. It follows that the manifest is insubstantial, mere appearance. And yet the socio, while drawing on the power of the mass or aggregation, gives full validity to appearance.

Yet, even though an entity is a part wrenched from the whole, the part loses none of the aspects of the original whole. Despite a change in scale, the microcosm retains all the components of the macrocosm. This idea fascinated Spinoza; it runs through psychology. An individual person thus comprises many other 'persons.' In this way, the bringing together of two is the aggregation of two 'manys' to form an inter-many. In every conversation, we hear, love or care for an echo in the other of 'many-in-one.' Democritus' view that an atom lies at the root of all things now gives way to the view that multiplicities lie at the root of the atom. The nature of an entity is a compound. When in psychology someone is said to be mad, it is assumed this is because they have multiple personalities, that they have internalised 'one-too-many.' People are deemed sane if they only contain 'many' personalities. It is difficult to avoid the conclusion that the combination of things is the explanation of things, that all the differences in the world do not need to cohere into one because they are already inter-connected. Multiplicity generates what is. But, where metaphysics points to the multiplicity in the universe, the socio points to it in human aggregation alone.

The ability of the socio to keep totality and particulars apart is aided by the disposition of humans to see themselves in others. The socio makes people say, in effect: 'When I think of myself I am already another.' Thus there is no need to think at the level of totality, only at the level of human aggregation. Philosophy acknowledges the power of truth to reveal the wholeness that lies behind all division. But truth is never brought to bear on the claim of human aggregation to be the sole vantage point from which to view the world. Whereas truth will show a binary divide to be obscuring a greater whole, the socio denies that the division between, say, the individual and society needs to be set in a greater whole. Instead both sides of the divide can be developed further, suspended and extended in glorious isolation from each other. This is saying more than that humans are contrary and prone to oppositional thinking. It goes beyond existentialism and postmodernism's claim that the more I am fully myself the more I escape societal coercion. The socio is saying: The more I am myself the more I notice I am the same as others. It can do this because all individuals are split. We may be judgemental about pleasure-seeking and deplore an absence of duty to others. But the socio tells us that our souls want both, that we are drawn to what we don't want, to that which harms or diminishes us, just as strongly as to that which we claim morally or physically uplifts us. I may want to smoke while knowing the dangers of smoking, and yet I go ahead. And I may harangue myself mercilessly for this urge and feel guilty. But nothing will stop me smoking because, by holding the two impulses in suspension, I stop the ideas that underpin the actions from engaging with each other. This split is the common ground between people. By keeping wants and moral judgement in different compartments, the split is allowed to stand for a fractured reality.

At this point we realise that what matters is not us humans, but what lies behind us. What lies behind us explains our erstwhile intellectual passivity. Richard Dawkins claims that we do what our genes want us to do, that is, to replicate. Humans are mere replication-machines. (He of course keeps God, or something beyond the genes, out of the picture.) Our view of humanity has switched. No longer can we rely on orthodox sets of values or directions of thought. What we fear most – death, illness, depression, guilt – can now be seen as our partners in life just as much as they might constitute our nemesis. When we ask what underpinned our lives when we were most true to ourselves (say in our 'teens and 'twenties) we might reply: to play with death by dabbling in intense experiences such as drugtaking, casual sex, high-living, addictive climbing of academic or professional greasy poles, fast-driving or dangerous sports. The socio is an attempt to explain why, when we address the 'big' things in life such as love, relationship, happiness, duty or purpose, we are drawn to and revulsed by them in equal measure. The resulting equivocation has found a place in Freud but not in philosophy. Metaphysics tells us that dichotomies are a foreshortening of wholeness. For example, life includes death because life is a big idea comprising many properties, one of which is death. Indeed, to be alive may not be to want to live: suicide is a major cause of death. Driving a car at excessive speed can be explained as a wish to experience life fully, but it also a dicing with death. We humans have so much energy or animation, yet we limit ourselves to what is respectable. Something has to give. That is what this shadowy side of life is. And yet we pretend we don't know this.

We must remember we are critiquing a process that potentially opens us to truth. The search for truth has to take account of the space occupied by the socio. The problem is not that the self is a multiplicity. Humanity also is a multiverse that hides many multiplicities. Yet we only get in touch with our 'own' multiplicity. Clearly the idea of self contains more than whatever is meant by 'oneself.' Philosophy is already familiar with the idea that the observer is like that which it observes. This leads to the notion that, if we turn our gaze back on ourselves, we will find the same as that which we claim to perceive in the world. This move underpins Hegel's view that the movement of history is a process in which mind will find (gaze back upon) itself. Broadly people see substance in terms of singularity, a move encouraged by Aristotle. This is not to suggest there is no essence, rather that the essence of essence is multiple. As we go in search of a core we find All. An 'other' in the sense that Levinas means it involves only me and someone else. What however if it is other to other? After all, the term 'process' is an hypothesis that the world is in constant flux. Indeed, metaphysics assumes we are the way the world is. Thales' 'All is water' can arguably be understood more profoundly when reversed. If we say 'Water contains the All' we can take this insight to be an attempt to make things heterogeneous, to conceptualise a totality that encompasses all differences. Entrapment in the socio arises from a failure to face indeterminacy squarely.

So, why not hypothesise that we already know what it means to know and that the epistemological details add nothing? Scientists seek knowledge of the origin of the universe and life. But Socrates famously said he knew that he did not know. Popper told us uncertainty is knowledge, that theories are not knowledge because they are constantly being replaced. We might now add that all we claim to know is the transient authenticity found in current narratives. The bind we get into is that, believing we lack formal knowledge, we end up worshipping forces we see as alien to ourselves; and all because we are full of life. This is the human; and this is reality as we've never accepted it. There may very well be something wrong about life but this is it. The socio tells us more about reality than we dare accept. We lower our gaze to focus on this or that part of it. And, in so doing, in this dichotomising move, we reveal more about ourselves than we find comfortable. The socio is saying there is a greater intimacy between consciousness (or humanity) and the world than we have realised. Platonic philosophy tells us we are already connected by primordial forces like love, forces that lead us away from individuation. But the socio tells us that we have never even emerged from primordiality, from an urge to do what the herd does. Humans will doggedly refuse to give up their vantage point upon things and adopt an Archimedean overview. Indeed, Leibowitz claims that will is not individual, that we join a larger cause in order to believe we are something.

The socio is the idea that lies behind society. There may be others and it might be hiding them. The socio may be the greatest influence on the way we live our lives. But it arises in the human realm; it only rivals reality because we let it do so. A simple way to reduce its power would be to clear our minds of what we take the mass of others to be thinking. There is no need to partake in a show of belonging to a mass; each of us already partakes in the whole, which is incomparably bigger than the mass. We can step away from compromising contact in order to relate cleanly to others. It is said that it takes two to tango, but philosophy says no, it only takes one. There is no need to dance with the people. We live life as a series of detachments from earlier bonds, finding ourselves the more so at each move. For sure, the grip of the social world is so powerful that strong measures are needed to loosen it. Zarathustra left the world for 10 years in order to gaze upon primordial nature before returning among people. Alternatively we can directly address unhelpful habits. We could say: Away with you, attraction and revulsion. Not only is my guilt about smoking really a fear of social rebuke, but the very smoking itself was a response to a social narrative about what people do in company. We can then avoid being revulsed by our erstwhile urge to smoke – or to fuse with the masses. The socio doesn't help with the greatest of questions: What is human possibility? But it gives us an example of what happens when thinking is left unexamined.

The preparedness of humans to abandon their liberty may be *the* philosophical question. A speedy resolution would be for each of us to say to the feelings that make us beholden to other people's opinions: I recognise that you are telling me something about reality but I won't be defined or guided by you. Then I will not, as a second move, have to pull back in horror from my rejection of you. I will not resort to the anxiety-creating manoeuvre of justifying my worship of the voice of the mass on the one hand and of atoning alone and often in despair on the other hand. We always have before us the inspiring example of Socrates' interlocutors who were prepared to let their entire mind-set be demolished under searching interrogation. But, whereas the Greeks were unafraid of wholeness and unpredictable movement, we today appear to be overwhelmed by both. Public kudos is given to whatever diverts us from wholeness – opinions, particularisation, action, good works, power, celebrity. We hold back from questioning the socio. Painful suspension between the Scylla of attraction and Charybdis of revulsion has not drawn a collective response. Socrates told us we can only do this ourselves. Before they entered the public square, Socrates' interlocutors realised they had to undergo the fiery baptism of a sustained personal interrogation. They realised that it only takes one to tango, that the urge to philosophise wells up from with. It cannot be induced by persuasion or attraction. It can never be a mass phenomenon because this points to the symbolic power of monarch or priest. The Greeks searched for the ideas hiding behind the apparent world, ideas which pivoted the mind towards the potentialities that lay behind all determinations and identities. We can now appreciate more fully the dilemma of the boy ignored by his mother.

The formation of an identity weakened his capacity to think. This issue is addressed in Part Three.

SUMMARY OF PART TWO

Part Two shows what happens when we adopt a non-philosophical approach to the human. The problem of the uneasy coexistence of consciousness and reality cannot be addressed. A split is created between the human and reality by the claims to reality of being, feelings, family, society and the socio. These intermediaries offer a false bridge; they refuse to admit that the two poles cannot meet. But postmodernism's contention that desire never possesses its object and epistemology never grasps ontology questions this move. Only philosophy helps us resolve the problem created when the flux of totality is solidified into two opposites, and one of the solidities (humans) reaches out to the other. Reaching for the truth, core or soul of the other is a philosophical move. We are generally very able to deal with the reality of the world as it emerges minute-by-minute. But we have yet to discover how to relate the mind to the world as a whole. We need to realise that by noticing differences arising second-by-second we are appreciating that otherness is actually sameness. Everything finds its place in the universe once we process what has happened; nothing extrudes or jars. By appreciating that there is no object to focus on, that there is only the process of exploring, we will have found otherness to be familiar. Life can be understood as an active process of knowing in which nothing is beyond our imagination. Connection between two - dialogue - is not the meeting of two minds or logi, but the traversing of one's own mind in the move towards the other. One can then harness the very energy of the other that at present is failing to relate to us. One doesn't reject this misplaced or dormant energy but rather accept it as part of the journey to otherness. Then one can stop seeking to incorporate the other. Instead, we can appreciate that we encounter the world only when we transcend the other as discrete entity.

This understanding is absent in all five claims. They highlight a problem. Consciousness has offered humans the chance to reconcile 'I am me' with 'I am not just me.' But this move has left us ungrounded in nature and not yet confident place-holders of ideas. So we hesitate. Instead of enabling the mind to process fresh thoughts, these five claims fill the mind with yet more dichotomies and content. Humans are left in a state of equivocation. The self is privileged over reality without noticing that, when we allow too much of the 'I' to come to the fore, we abandon our essence. We engage less with the in-between. None of the claims recognises that one's essence lies in otherness. When we ricochet back and forth between self and essence it becomes difficult to resolve this split in our soul. The Greeks would have said that our dilemma is that, although we are essentially social, we have incorporated into society the 'I' that makes society such a problematic enterprise. In short, we have not yet learned to handle the consciousness with which we have been endowed. If we take it, as did the ancients, that the in-between is a force that precedes society and politics and reveals the universe to us, we could resolve the issue by throwing ourselves wholeheartedly into society. But even as we did this we would have to hold firm to our default position, which is that society is underpinned by the in-between. But society cleaves staunchly to the 'I' or self, while genuflecting towards the in-between and the world at large.

The Greeks turned to the idea of the One and the Many to unravel the problematic of human relationship. They started with two hypothesises: that the One (society) comprises in-between forces that precede the state and politics, and that only philosophy can excavate the in-between from beneath the superstructure of significations and identities that comprise the self. So we need a system of society and governance that builds on the in-between rather than denies or supplants it. How then can a system be developed in which one person (of the Many) can relate to the mass or totality of all people (the One)? This question relates directly to the issue of citizenship that was so close to Socrates' heart. How can a single person, preoccupied with their own issues (self-absorption), take a disinterested part in the governance of the polis? If they were overwhelmed by their own issues (which an addiction to heightened feelings, a failure to disengage from the family, or a submission to unquestioned social imperatives might cause) there is a danger they'd view public life as a way of dealing with unresolved inner strife. The within of a self-absorbed person would triumph at the expense of people at large, people whose deepest impulses were moved by the in-between. This is what happens when people enter the political arena before submitting to a Socratic interrogation. Had they done so they would have realised that friendship between two discrete individuals is possible only by invoking the idea of friendship. Metaphysics and daily life move as one. This move also applies to politics. Citizens would be able to relate to the polis both as an idea and a matter of contiguous living.

All five cases treat humans as the measure of all things. Humans are left to follow where their unexamined minds will take them. They search merely for a human purchase on reality. Wholeness, the interpersonal or the in-between have given way to particularity and personhood. People are drawn to figments of the mind, to fragments of the whole. But Socrates expected citizens to handle an encounter with anyone who came across their horizon, and especially with someone they had avoided hitherto. The Greek term agape means the ability to engage with everyone, in other words, with everything that is non-me. This is another way of expressing otherness. Socrates advocated a form of universalism. No one need feel compelled to take the role of personal hero amidst a crowd of non-heroes, as in existentialism, because a rising tide would lift all. A mind that is unafraid of entering this territory would have little difficulty with the process of conceptualising. But we must look elsewhere for such minds.

This search takes us to six more claims to be the avatars of the human. In Part Three, psychosis, God (of the philosophers), ideas, speech, friendship, and the public space known as the Agora take a different tack from those in Part Two. They pivot the mind away from the self towards the space of the in-between.

PART THREE: A MIND THAT IS ABLE TO REFLECT

CHAPTER NINE: THE HUMAN EMERGES IN PSYCHOSIS

'The modern schizophrenic...is a mind bared to his environment, waiting on gods in a godless world.' Julian Jaynes, *The Origin of Consciousness in the Breakdown of the Bicameral Mind.*

As Jaynes suggests above, psychosis is an open and frank engagement with the world. (I treat the term philosophically here, not pathologically.) We must step back for a moment and recall that philosophical method loosens up thinking by pivoting it towards the absolute. It takes all statements to the meta where their claims to ontological status are equalised. At the meta we can leave contentions aside and focus on the essence that lies behind the clash of opinions. Humans can now return to the connected-up world. But Plato also had in mind that, at this very juncture, the world would reconnect to itself. This means that the bifurcating move of consciousness would be cancelled out and everything would find its place in harmony. Plato is telling us there is something at the core or essence that is receptive to everything.

In this chapter I hypothesise that this core is psychosis and that it is the ontology of the human. I take neurosis to be merely the layers of guilt, recrimination, remorse and doubt that have been added to the core. In philosophical terms neurosis focuses on appearance because it is associated with the emergence of the self. Socrates' response to this situation was to peel away and dispose of the superimposed layers. Imagine for a moment meeting another person and not being sure how to respond to them. On the one hand you can reach out to the social code and be civil and polite. In this case you will have let the id collapse. This move detaches you from reality. This is the neurotic position. On the other hand you could collapse the superego, which is the barrier to the id. Now the id can fully engage with the world. This is the psychotic position. The point I am making is that psychosis opens humans to the abundance of the world; neurosis responds to needy, doubting thoughts about it.

Psychology tells us that, when things go wrong, they go wrong inside a person's mind. However, this conclusion fails to understand Plato's point that consciousness is the regulation of the space between people. Psychology creates the neurotic disposition when it puts this relational space into the individual mind. Freud was a profound philosopher in other respects, but he was a sociologist and not a philosopher of the mind. The in-between is the genuine article. Deleuze describes it (qua schizophrenia) as normality. But Freud's influence is still strong. All the same, we need only remove the notion of an interior mind and the blockage to a relationship with others vanishes. Nonetheless, given the bad habits that have built up over time, this may be easier said than done.

We must go back in time to set the context. The appearance of being is the beginning of history. Being arose from the emergence of consciousness which allowed humans to reflect on their thoughts. But then, and this is the cataclysmic event, consciousness retreated into itself. Two viable avenues were open to consciousness: either to be used to develop a sense of being or to be used as the vehicle of thought. Humanity's fall occurred at this point. It took neither of these avenues; instead it settled in a state of intransigence. It fell from being and from the world into a realm of dualism and separation. Philosophy emerged against this backdrop. It understood that consciousness is in the world and that, in our essence, we are consciousness. But it also realised we have personally commandeered consciousness and confined it within our minds. This is the crucial aspect of the Fall - we have privatised thought. The outcome is that there is no relationship between consciousness and the world. It is in response to this dilemma that philosophy evolved the idea of the 'meta.' This enables us to use consciousness to enquire about the world while also enquiring into consciousness itself. The key breakthrough occurred when we realised that consciousness submits itself to scrutiny, even as it scrutinises the world. Out of this realisation emerged philosophical method - to think about thinking. But this method, which arose most clearly in Plato, did not survive Aristotle's attack on its tendency to infinite regress (to think about something and think about that thinking, and then about the previous series of thought, ad nauseam). The answer to Aristotle's criticism is that regression does not take place once we direct thinking towards totality. This is the meta. There is nowhere further to regress to. But philosophy has remained stuck ever since at

Aristotle's rebuttal of Plato. Nevertheless the meta allowed Plato to pursue his idea of humanity's return to the world. This is not a return to our personal roots, or tribal or other origins, which would be a response to the yearnings of the soul. It is a journey inspired by the muse and provoked by thought; a journey of the mind. It is about the possibility of humanity engaging with the world instead of conquering it. Most humans live within themselves and not the world. We believe we will collapse without defences to protect us from a reputedly dangerous world.

The individual mind has expanded to incorporate the whole world. Everything that approaches this inner world must conform to it. Selves must strive to connect to others from this base, with the promise that this will resolve all the problems. But all that happens is that two worlds collide or collapse into each other. When we bring Plato back into the picture we can see that connection is not an answer to aloneness. The Platonic move is to let go of the idea of aloneness altogether. Then we can set about creating an in-between that takes away the two individuals' need to search for meaning or purpose in each other or in their coupledom. Of course the creation of an in-between can take the form of a baby. But a profound philosophical reading of this move is to see the relationship itself as the focus. This may take the form of a common project that raises the couple's gaze beyond individual neediness. But it can become more than this when we understand that the relationship is the in-between. It needs no further embellishment. It generates possibilities beyond the present ken of the couple. We don't need to look far for guidance - classical works of culture have drawn deep from the well of the in-between.

At the heart of the in-between is overflowing abundance. We are familiar with the generativity of nature. And of course we may focus within it on the survival of the fittest, the chance element that lets some rise and others perish. But a bigger point to notice is the sheer generosity of nature: so many seeds are produced so that a single seed can put down its roots. Nature just throws off its all with abandon. Humanity on the other hand seeks to stem this flow, as Freud well knew, by imposing a working principle on it.

On the other hand we could trust the flow to do its job (wastage notwithstanding). By opening to the infinity of imagination we can handle our cautionary, panicky and hesitating tendencies. The Greek idea of the Agora (a public space for discussions) is a case in point. There, everyone facilitated the development of others. People were an inspiration to each other. As catalysts they released energy which broke down the floodgates holding back their potential, floodgates which their doubts and rectitude had hitherto erected. The Agora obviated a tendency to fear things getting out of hand.

The psychosis/neurosis discourse hides a confusion about the capability of consciousness. Nature does not recognise its own abundance; only consciousness does this. Yet, once we are aware of nature's abundance, our minds immediately view it negatively, as something with the power to escape our control. Put another way, consciousness opens us to the wonder of the world a split second before doubt floods our mind. When we become aware of the flow of the universe our very appreciation of it is made impossible. In philosophical or theological terms this phenomenon appears as the impossibility of looking into the face of God. But philosophy says: Don't despair. The outcome is not foregone; we only expect mutual destruction because we we've sunk into despair. A full human does not arise at the expense of others or of something else. A thoroughgoing encounter with another human is within reach. But we need to gain enough distance from the immediacy of the situation to contextualise it while not losing a sensitivity to its nuances. The application of philosophical method to our use of consciousness is the only approach that is free of mind-distortions. It will demand all our courage, skill, patience and commitment. The alternative is to collapse into a nihilistic belief that ignorance is bliss. By raising our thoughts to the realm of metaphysical abstraction we can see what lies behind these human yearnings. We can see that consciousness is seeking engagement with the world and the world seeking to be recognised by consciousness.

Psychosis underpins the human. We are all psychotics beneath the social skin. It is only the urge to classify humans into manageable groups that suggests we are otherwise. By hiding us from our underlying disposition this move has the effect of making people run away from the psychotic in them. The refusal to accept psychosis as the underpinning of humans takes us to the heart of society. It is believed, and psychology propagates this view, that we develop attachment to mother or key carer in the first two years of life. Yet attachment is implicit in the human. Indeed the first two years can best be understood in terms of detachment. Every hesitation, show of annoyance, and negative movement of the eyelid is a sign to the baby that its route is away from the mother. In other words, psychosis arises in connection. The completion of the Oedipal development throws the neurotic into the world to form an identity in an act of separation. This is the typical move. Yet it has taken us away from an enjoyment of abundance, as Old Testament writers and Heidegger remind us. But the psychotic remains attached and reveals, as AN Whitehead has pointed out, that relationships are ontological entities.

Psychosis is base mode. Neurosis is a collapse from this base. Needless to say, there is no essential difference between people. There are only different intensities. Yet society and the intellectual hierarchy are neurotic and want to split hairs and expand small differences. The neurotic is defended against the world yet doesn't want to know it. The psychotic on the other hand doesn't want to run away from other humans or the world, even at the risk of violence or death. But philosophy puts these differences aside in a search for the big picture. It helps us understand these dichotomies. The philosophical move is to realise that there is no fundamental difference between each of us; indeed there is no 'me.' It all boils down to the method we use to generate ideas.

Why then do we distinguish between humans? Why do we categorise people? After all, thinking at the meta or absolute tells us that everything has its place in wholeness. Wholeness can understand and adapt to everything. There is no need to categorise humans in terms of their appearance or behaviour, be it rational or irrational. If rationality is deemed an absolute idea it must include everything. Otherwise it is a partial idea that pertains to the mind, self and epistemology. It cannot be both. So, if we conjecture, for the sake of it, that 1% of the population are psychotics and 1% are lawyers, where lies the difference? Psychotics 'do' psychosis; they practise psychosis as well as lawyers practise law. There is no inherent core that includes lawyers and excludes psychotics. Yet, as Foucault argues, we (or society) do not extend inclusion in the core to madness, criminality or sexuality. The mad are only different from the non-mad when we start categorising people. Yet categorising is an attempt to hold together a world that is deemed to be fragmented. No, we are all afloat in the flow or flux, in indeterminacy. When we raise psychosis to the meta we equalise all attempts to privilege one particularity over another. The concept of psychosis underpins the human. Humanity's openness to the world means we are all psychotics.

CHAPTER TEN: THE HUMAN EMERGES WHEN STANDING BEFORE GOD

"To break idolatry, not to sanction values which stem from human drives and interests - that is faith.' Yeshayahu Leibowitz, *Accepting the Yoke of Heaven*.

Psychosis is an opening to truth and reality, but not the only one. Openness is also at the heart of the idea of God. God is an absolute or totality in which humans find a place. In this chapter I use Yeshayahu Leibowitz's ideas to construe God (although the God of the philosophers and not a transcendent Being) as the totality we deny when we worship idols. An idol is a self-serving human depiction of the world. It diverts us from the search for truth and reality. Each dialogue in Plato is about the removal of an idol. Implicit in the notion of an idol is a fear that 'the devil finds work for idle hands,' that, left to themselves, humans slip into troublesome ways. The devil is human self-regard which treats personal experience as the measure of all things. Unable to fight the devil by ourselves, we must bind ourselves to a post, to something steadfast. Otherwise relationships between humans will be trivial, clingy or conflictual, or sheer impossible. Indeed other people will become idols to us if we view them in a romantic or exaggerated way. In *The Four Loves* CS Lewis famously depicts friends quietly conversing as they sit side by side looking out at the world, and erotic lovers struggling to handle the intensity of looking directly into each other's eyes. In the latter case, a relationship between two independent individuals has been replaced by the bondage or fusion of two needy selves.

Leibowitz claims that, without God, we are only capable of living a trivialised, idol-worshipping life. He is saying that God is essential if we are to upgrade friendship from its common-or-garden level to that of the in-between. But he is also saying that God stands outside reality, that He does not exist. He is an idea. So, if we are to stand before Him, we must admit we do not exist. We are an idea. The worship of idols not merely trivialises life, it misreads the notion of an idea. To be an idea is to be divine. A fall from this state takes us into a pit of fragile self-regard. In the era of mythos the polytheistic gods were an expression of the self. But, during the Axial Age, God emerged as love and the self as the chief idol. Love is a quest after reality or truth. An idol obstructs this quest. In brief, the problem for humanity is its own narcissism.

People yearn for cosmic connection. But when they cannot satisfy this yearning they transfer it onto constructs or objects. A yearning for cosmic connection now becomes a want for specific objects - a lover, a shiny car, even a supply of chocolate bars - that promise to mitigate the general yearning. People have turned inwards, away from the world. But this turn inward to the self has let them down. Because it cannot critique itself it denies reality; it seeks to hold together a shaky internal congruence. It tries to colonise anything that threatens to disturb the fragility of this congruence. In addition, an uncritical use of mind has allowed it to shatter wholeness into fragments. Fragments lack an anchor in the universe. The mind responds by privileging some fragments above others. The preferred fragments appear to offer redemption from the judgements of the world, and so we idolise them. We believe we cannot live without them. Even believing in God to excess turns Him into an idol, as the story of Job testifies. It needs a serious disturbance to challenge our habitual thinking. Yet, once idols are destroyed and the bubble bursts, a space is exposed. This is God, reality or truth. The notion of a space concealed by idol-worship is found in the Greek conviction that sense impressions are not to be trusted. Reality itself doesn't need changing; what gets in the way of engaging with it is in the eye of the beholder. It is in Nietzsche's fear that the space left by the death of God is already being filled with the idols of reason, being, history, grammar, and belief in the senses. John Caputo's postmodern theology treats the name of God as an idol. Caputo points to the name of God as a placeholder where claims to certainty, such as those promised by signification, are encased. Leibowitz suggests that the silence of God since Moses has created a vacuum which idols rush to fill. He adds however that, though humans have the intelligence and the will to understand this situation, they simply don't want to know.

An idol is a metaphor for the development of a personal inner life. This is what happens when we fail to direct our gaze away from ourselves. When our passions are inflamed or when we obsess over a thought we take ourselves to be wanting, to be missing something. Beneath a display of bravado we feel inadequate, diminished in the company of others, overawed or unsupported. We see other people as speaking with confidence and drowning us out. In this situation we seek whatever compensation or diversion we can find by erecting idols.

Yet, when we let go of fear of emptiness and resist the temptation to erect an idol, the empty space becomes pregnant with untold possibilities. Indeed, shouldn't we welcome being overridden by others? This situation is only showing us that the person who overrides us is needy (something that is usually seen as lovably human), that life is often unfair and, not just that this is alright, but that we can handle it without too much effort. The plea is to kill all inner certainties, the valorisation of feelings, wants, needs, preferences and experiences. These are the true idols. Only God is certain, so when we seek for certainty we are acting as if God has migrated inside us. We should not take our presumptions seriously. If anything we should dance around them. What, have we become a God that we know things with certainty? Has our thinking shifted from a fascination with metaphors to a conversion of thoughts into idols? And doesn't an idol or concretised thought really seek to be free, to stop being obvious and immediate, and to explore the universe, reality, essence and truth in the way that philosophical method allows? When idols transform into metaphors again they become devices capable of carrying us to the absolute. Our personal experience may serve our ego well but it can only ever reveal one aspect of things. It will never yield enduring truth.

Leibowitz's diagnosis of the dilemma of humanity focuses on the impossibility of handling forces beyond its control. Nonetheless, although nature no longer offers a guide to action, humans are blessed with a will that can channel desire away from the self into beneficent communal enterprises. Leibowitz's God is absolutely incomparable to any form of reality we could possibly encounter. God's radical transcendence allows us to cast a light on the nature of humankind. The same thought is found in Caputo's association of the idea of God with that of the event. An event not only emerges from past conditions but also contains a germ of the future. It is dynamic, builds upon itself, arcs back to prior stages and makes detours that can only be explained post hoc. Yet the event still retains human traces, for it pertains to the individual mind. Leibowitz would see this as letting human affairs enter the scene. God is the only divinity; nothing pertaining to the world or accessible to the human mind, be it humans, nature, or even the idea of reality, is divine. So, where philosophy has placed reality beyond humankind, Leibowitz places God beyond both the human and reality. He believed science will one day understand reality and will thoroughly 'humanise' it. In polytheist Greece nature was worshipped: there were gods of the seas, the heavens, and the wind. But monotheism placed divinity in the one God. Spinoza got round nature's claim to be divine (and so rival God) by collapsing God into nature. But Leibowitz settles for no half-measures. Not merely is there only one God but there has been no God to appeal to since Moses, he says. Yet God's absence makes our need to commit to the idea of Him even greater. Everything else is but idol worship.

Will emerges in the space vacated by nature. It is a drive that can be directed away from the self to God. This is an echo of Plato, where a desire such as love can be harnessed to reason and placed in the realm of metaphysics. We can go further and add Socrates' Agora spirit to Plato's concern for the training of future citizens and say, like Durkheim, that God is the communal. Thus a desire like love connects us ultimately to the communal. And the communal is human greatness. In Greek, 'Aga' is the first syllable of both Agora and agape. Both are exercises that transfer attention from the self to the totality of other people, respectively in a gathering of all adults in the public square and of love that is not confined to one or a select few. But Leibowitz makes a radical move now, by directing movement from God or the communal to the human. This move reverses the common assumption that movement flows from the human to God or the communal. Now both human expressions, wanter and wanted or lover and beloved, can be seen as two aspects of the human. Knowing God now involves a transcendence of human desire. The human receives God's bounty - wholeness, truth - without needing to grasp for it. Reaching beyond the self or the human is the first philosophical move. It asks us to stop trying to understand things in human terms, whether as feelings, definitions or idols, and to desist from placing desire in a self, an object, or a poetic paean to love, simply because these placements are so familiar to us. Thinking in human terms always needs God or the muse if it is to reacquire movement. The fullest explanation of the human, such as mapping the brain, will never take us there. Instead we are asked to metamorphose ourselves rather than our desire or the desired object, and to see everything through God's eyes. We are asked to bring ourselves up and not God down. Philosophy reaches to the skies, beyond all that is familiar to us. It takes us to reality or God.

What does this say about humans? Leibowitz deduces that humankind has no nature other than that which constitutes the search for one itself. The search takes the human to a place where he or she can stand before God. The problem is that humans possess animation beyond what would be sufficient for other creatures while at the same time displaying little volition with which to direct this animation. In addition to this characteristic of humans, the human condition seems to include a propensity to love that which is unattainable. This disposition can easily lead to disillusion and ennui. Nonetheless Leibowitz suggests that this disposition cannot be staunched. Equally humans are not capable of learning from knowledge. What we know doesn't alter our behaviour. All we do is to respond to our drives and will. Humankind has generally taken our drives to be object-oriented. Indeed philosophy endorses this view. Yet ontology has bedazzled us. We have fallen into thinking that an epistemological search must lead to an object or conclusion. Ontology can now be seen as an idol. All we can say is that humans are striving animals who are capable of acts of goodness.

What then can we do with what we are? Leibowitz elevates will to become the star in the human firmament. The possession of will means we are not a thing like other creatures. Will drives our behaviour even though it is not justifiable in absolute terms. It can act in any way without rationale. Humans do not live according to nature. Whereas a thing follows its nature, we follow what we want. We thereby become a want. We are in the realm of ethics, as understood as 'you are what you want.' But faith frees us from the downward pull of idolatry and raises our gaze to the Good. Good lies in the realm of God beyond nature. Leibowitz takes up Aristotle's suggestion that goodness offers humans a purpose that manifests in cooperative ventures of great mutual benefit.

Leibowitz says that humans seek a place to stand before God. But, what does this mean? Firstly, let us not forget that God stands outside all human drives and interests. So, to stand there saves us from being ensnared in appearance. This is a version of the Greek message that philosophy is a clearing-away exercise. Secondly, the issue is not to grasp something but to remove the blockage that hides what is already here. The blockage is created when the human clings to a self. The analogy of Plato's Cave stands for any construction thrown up by human consciousness. Thirdly, in Leibowitz's words, meaning arises from goodness, for which faith clears the way. And faith is a pivot away from narcissism. It is an orientation that steps beyond human constructions of the world. The echoes of Plato are loud and clear. But those of Aristotle are even louder. Leibowitz reverses the usual human relation to God so that He is a means to an end. God is now an idea. We can think about God without having to ask if He exists. God is the epitome of thinking. One can say: I think so there is God. One is committed to thinking itself, not to God as a transcendent Being. He will never appear and can be construed as make-believe. And moreover, the human commitment to the idea of God as thought must never waver if goodness is to be attained.

I have used Leibowitz's view of a commitment to God to emphasise the centrality in philosophy of the commitment to consciousness. Commitment is not too strong a word because thought is the sine qua non of philosophy. God as the object of thinking presents an entity about which one thinks. This is also of course Plato's initial move. His starting point is the dichotomous way we view the world (it is there and I am here). He then reveals the space within this gap to be the source of a movement that not only underpins the universe but is the universe. Hereby division gives way to difference, and difference between things gives way to the idea of difference itself. In other words, Plato returns us from particulars to universals, from constructs of thought to concepts. For Leibowitz, God refers to the is-ness that lies beyond reality. Leibowitz is telling us that our task is to investigate the relation of the human to is-ness.

Thinking restores movement to reality. It curtails the common human addiction to soul-searching and takes us out of our known world. Consciousness flows from a human towards an object. That the object is imaginary is of no account. The flow, orientation or movement is all. Once movement occurs, the need to posit a subject or an object disappears. These dichotomous notions are merely stimuli to movement. They arise because humans believe themselves to be separated from everything around them – until they orient their thinking towards the world. We can see that consciousness is the human pivot towards a nature or first object that will never be found. This move is sufficient unto itself. The search is all; it is generative.

We must return to the idea of a gap between human and world, whence there emerges a fundamental impulse for life, animation and movement. Humankind's pursuit is not an attempt to address subject, object or reality but to place humankind before God or consciousness. Something emerges that has not hitherto manifested but has nonetheless driven us to feel and strive. It is the idea of the in-between that creates movement between two entities. This is Plato's search for Form. It is what arises when we stand before God in Leibowitz's thought. It is existentialism's concern with the longing, dread, and anxiety that fill the unconscious. But in the latter case existentialism subtly takes us away from consciousness and makes everything a personal matter. This defeats any attempt to commit to movement beyond the human.

Leibowitz re-emphasises the idea of movement. Everything is in process of development, the very development that idolatry attempts to block. It is a short move from Leibowitz's 'development' to the 'in-between' in Greek thought. Thought is the in-between that opens up a connection. Here is the genesis of movement.

The God of the philosophers is reality plus all that has been left out of reality. We are not required to change anything in order to stand before God. But we are asked to think about all the manifestations and ramifications of this encounter. A move that takes us beyond our usual sense of the human does not involve us in exploring some kind of non-human or wholly natural state. But it does involve us in thinking of a human free of all presuppositions and preoccupations. This space is not 'harmonious' in the modern sense, where things can be fitted into an existing field after a process of adjustment. Rather it is a space that can itself adjust to include all things: warts, sharp edges and all. It amounts to the enfolding or embracing of the seemingly most alien or unacceptable. It doesn't smother, distort, or judge. Things remain themselves in their entirety.

Now we are able to approach God by invoking the idea of process. The content of what is said by individual members of a group can be ignored; it doesn't create process, flow or interaction. These latter arise from the spaces in-between the contributions: the changing tenor, the nuanced and changing relations between thoughts and feelings in a gathering where the group itself acts as a member. And yet, in an important sense, that things are said matters because the more anyone speaks the more they empty their minds of the content that excites and disturbs the soul. We can posit a point being reached where everything takes place outside the human psyche. The outside is God. Or, the absence of inner clutter is God. There is no counterpoint or standard of comparison between inner and outer now because there is no inside. God is simply the absence of idols.

Another approach is to see God as the communal. In Socrates' model of human interaction the communal and the idea of process elide. Love of God happens when we connect the community to the drive behind our desires. But we must reverse what we take to be the usual direction of movement. Instead of wanter seeking the wanted, both can now be fused into will, because both are the human component. It is this that relates to God. To love God is now a matter of receiving and not of giving. We are able to acknowledge that we have always been receiving the beneficence of wholeness, truth and God. Knowing God involves entering into a process of knowing that can be better expressed as living in the knowing of God. We apply ourselves to knowing in the certainty that we will never arrive at full knowledge.

Only now can we truly start to live. We can do whatever we want. What does it matter that we lack a 'human nature' when we are metaphysical entities? We metaphorically float in the air and can be tethered to anything, idols included of course! Humans can decide to stop eating, sleeping or procreating. Some have changed sex. Acts of great idealism astonish us. Endurance and speed records topple. Technology marches on. But more pertinently, nothing need bind us to our self. If we are creatures of anything it is consciousness. But consciousness waits for us to discover it the more! We have overtaken nature and can use will to find personal fulfilment and confer public benefaction. We need never fear losing our self, becoming something else, or moving closer to others. For the loss of the self clears the ground for the human to emerge as a concept.

CHAPTER ELEVEN: THE HUMAN EMERGES AS A CONCEPT

'But what if man had eyes to see the true beauty – the divine beauty, I mean, pure and clear and unalloyed, not clogged with the pollutions of mortality and all the colors and vanities of human life – thither looking, and holding converse with the true beauty simple and divine? Remember how in that communion only, beholding beauty with the eye of the mind, he will be enabled to bring forth, not images of beauty, but realities (for he has hold not of an image but of a reality) and bringing forth and nourishing true virtue to become the friend of God and immortal, if mortal man may.' Plato, *Symposium*.

The emergence of logos (conceptual thought) gave humans the means to 'real-ise' life; to return themselves to reality. When the Greeks discovered the mind (or consciousness) they placed it outside humans, sensing that there is no such thing as mind except in its metaphorical usage. It is an organising principle or method that lies ready to be called upon by the human. A metaphorical return to wholeness occurs when humans use this method - to think about thinking, or to take up philosophy. Socrates integrated the complexity of the human into the external world such that we are now able to realise that philosophy creates the world. The world is not there otherwise. Human yearning has culminated in a love of ideas or God. This realisation can give birth to a community of enquirers. In these communities relationships (the in-between) release movement from the trammels of the self. The soul is at ease when there are no rules to tell us what to think and do. Uninhibited process releases is-ness. Conversely we halt the movement inherent in the metaphor of mind when we take up a position or make a doctrinal or dogmatic claim. When we accept the world as appearance we know the mind has taken up a position. We know that movement has stalled.

Reality is not consciousness itself but the product of consciousness. We can only address the world through consciousness but we are left having to deal with the dualisms that consciousness creates. Philosophy addresses these dualisms the better to address the impression they give of a crack or barrier having been erected between humans and reality. So, starting in life, philosophy takes life's issues to metaphysics where life's cracks can be understood.

The Greeks claimed that everything that has been fractured by the mind is already in the process of returning to source; that is, to the source of all things, source itself, and not one of many. At the source a thing finds its rightful place among all things. The interrelation of things starts to emerge when we question dualisms. First, the fulcrum of thought is moved beyond dichotomous thinking. Now thinking sets out on a journey towards reality. The very process of reorientation begins to reveal the relational nature of a thing; it subsists in what I call the in-between. This is the Platonic return to source. The source can be approached either from its origin (Plato) or its telos or completion (Aristotle). For example, take the sentence 'I feel bad.' Its fulcrum is the verb 'feel' which denotes movement, emergence or becoming. It is more real than the two poles either side of it, which connote an unmoving one-on-one, subject-object relationship. The 'I' and 'bad' derive meaning only from the verb 'feel.' They are particularities that attempt to arrest movement, snapshots that try to stop time moving. In common speech they are given primacy. But the Greeks realised that if we downgrade them and elevate the verb we will allow reality to emerge. The verb is thus the in-between, the gap between two notional things. We are now free to attach ourselves to whatever system of thought or belief we choose because they are just that, systems of thought or belief. They are not ontological. We have resisted the pressure of language to cling to determinacy. When Plato said that things only exist when we think about them he was referring to the movement generated between people. He was saying that humans are yet to be born! They are presently nothing more than a claim to be real. But Plato was also questioning the status of reality for, if human are waiting to be born, the same process of emergence must apply to minute-by-minute reality. Both are completely open questions.

The first tremors of change were felt among the hunter gatherers who roamed the earth millennia ago. Some worshipped myths about the features in their lives they most feared, admired or valued. War, death, the oceans and the stars were given superhuman status. At the heart of this mythology was a primordial conflict between humans and all things non-human. When the storyteller left for the next village the listeners would pore over the questions raised by tales of battling heroes, shipwrecks and escapes from monsters. The villagers questioned, hypothesised, conjectured and eventually learned to create concepts around the biggest issues such as life, goodness, beauty, truth and reality. The gap between humankind and things was now a space pregnant with questions. The process we call philosophy was born. As the profundity of the questions deepened the questioners began to doubt what they had previously taken for granted. Arguments could no longer be clinched by reference to a thing's concretion or physicality; a 'thing's' utility was seen to offer an inadequate inkling as to its potential. The seemingly anchored notions of human and thing faded into obscurity as attention switched to the conversations in the space that had been freed up. Concepts subsumed everything that hitherto possessed a claim to solidity or definition. It became clear that is-ness is concealed and that reality is but a concept. Plato was asking us to conceive of life beyond human experience. We are asked to upgrade our imagination, because reality is indeed imaginary. Thinking about reality is no longer an option because reality is thought.

Humans are only a gaze. Yet there is no one behind it. A gaze is merely someone opening themselves to the world outside them. Consciousness is now the sixth sense. The eyes absorb light. Consciousness absorbs ideas. It notices, prioritises and organises them.

If we possessed only a body we would, of course, be like other creatures. But our capacity to think throws aside all notions based on the animal kingdom. This capacity is a boon beyond comparison. But the human response to it is mostly one of puzzlement and confusion. The word 'thought' denotes the ability of a human to reflect beyond the limits of their own experience. A thinking being can be said to have transcended itself, to have perceived itself as part of a greater whole. This is a source of wonder: knowledge can be gained, viewpoints broadened and scenarios imagined. Unfortunately however, the thinking process has a life of its own. Once started it seems incapable of stopping. It thinks about an object, then about itself thinking about the object, and then about itself thinking about itself thinking, and so on. Life becomes a hall of mirrors and incapacity sets in. A gift has become a nightmare. The capacity to think is indeed the greatest gift, but until it is used judiciously it is also a cruel one.

So yes, we can say that we are animals that can reflect. But when we start to look more closely at this statement we enter a cul-de-sac. Who or what is doing the thinking? Is it the person or is it thought itself? Is thought a thing-in-itself, a force or process in which humans merely partake? In any case, how does a human distinguish between thinking about, for instance, a sense perception of a flower and thinking about this very thought? Which is real? Does the second move take thought to a more profound level, or does it only complicate matters?

This point can be expressed another way. Animals are said to possess a nature determined by their place in the scheme of things. But the possession of a capacity to think carries humans beyond this state. Their imaginative powers make it impossible to tie them down to a state of concretion or predictability. But if they have no nature what are they? We have returned to the same question. The Greeks responded to this dilemma by stopping the reflective process after the first two moves. A human thinks about reality and then thinks about the earlier thought, and then no more. Thought is now in process. The task becomes one of exploring and understanding thought and not replicating the process endlessly. To activate this kind of thinking is to open a door into another world. Here, hypotheses can be explored and the imagination offered space to roam. But the second move was radical. The Greeks contended that it is possible to think metaphysically only when we stop imposing reason on consciousness.

Humans are a problematic entity. There is a gap between what we are and what we think we are. This problem can be resolved simply by dropping what we think we are. We would gain by this move because what we think we are is dominantly the product of negative experiences. Of course, as we know, people generally tend to hang on to their burdens. Alternatively we could hail the way we are by essentially letting good friends' uplifting view of us prevail.

As an abstraction or an illusion of concreteness we are not in the world. We only engage with the world when we conceptualise. At core we are an idea in the realm of essence or truth. When we shed all explanations we are but a witness of the world. On the surface we may purvey narratives about ourselves as bus drivers or nurses. But we are capable of going beneath the surface and simply witnessing things. I look at you but know you are a subject looking at me as an object. Even pebbles respond to gravity, water, and other pebbles. Nothing is passive; all is active, but only in ways that thinking can evince.

When we bring God in from outside and make Him a force within humanity we arrive at the idea of consciousness. At the core of consciousness sits active perception. Our turning attention to things is us. Pivoting, perceiving, attending - this is a human's nature. Perception is seminal. Just as the idea precedes the physical so logos or thought is perception before it comes into being as energy or matter. The nature of a thing is its logos. The more we listen and perceive the more we can tell ourselves we know ourselves. But we are actually paying attention to the world. Certainly, as we listen, we discover our feelings and can think they are us. Yet we are capable of taking things to another level. There we are not bound by anything. Our ability to think means we can do the opposite of anything we presently choose to do. There is always an alternative.

Put another way, we create reality; we don't discover it. It follows our decisions. Humans are in the realm of is-ness, but most of the time, maybe even without knowing it, certainly without questioning it, humans can be said to reside in the realm of the ought, the injunction. A collapse into ethics notwithstanding, we do not belong anywhere material such as a land, nation or clan. Materiality does not confine us. We are ultra-real, beyond reality. This is what residing in the realm of is-ness means. Reality is a response to God, the muse or inspiration. For sure it offers a vaster context than existence into which to place the human. But God is outside reality - and so are we. By placing ourselves with God outside reality we are able to create magnificent things and experience ourselves creating these things. This is humanity in the world. Leibowitz calls it the will expressing faith. It manifests as a human unity, as a coordinated communal effort.

Having acquired consciousness, we can do anything. No longer does nature configure our behaviour. History is the unfolding of the sum total of our choices such as group decisions, social movements and so on. There is no inevitability about it. It is not independent of mind. But will is the dominant force in it. Needless to say, we are doomed to watch a la Heraclitus as wills collide. Life adds together many elements of animation or thought such as facts, quantum physics, and inanimate objects that act as if they are disconnected from nature.

Our devotion to people, ideas or projects creates a parallel universe. Belief is the basis of human endeavour.

Leibowitz was adamant that no amount of knowledge will change it. So, everything derives from goodness. That is to say, what we think is right, not what underpins rightness. The world is not anchored in 'that is the case,' but in belief (God). Belief equates to something outside reality as we know it. Genesis tells us God is there before Paradise: 'In the beginning God created the heavens and the earth.' How do we cope with this? It is outside our conception - we can conceive of reality but not its beginning. There is something beyond what we conceive with our limited consciousness. The idea of God reminds us there is something beyond what we can conceive - faith - that supports us as we reach outside reality.

Thought begins in reality and creates hypotheses of a realm outside reality. Now we are God possessing a capacity to generate human endeavour, relate collectively, and make things happen that will not have happened otherwise. This cannot occur in the realm of nature. People often believe things can be explained in physical terms. But philosophy tells us: no, when we apply ourselves to things we go beyond the physical. But we're responsible for these endeavours. Existentialism exhorts us to stand by what we've created. Our will is not arbitrary; but we're responsible for it all the same. Even as an idea the human must still show courage and commitment.

CHAPTER TWELVE: THE HUMAN EMERGES FROM SPEECH

'The Greeks have but one word Logos, for both Speech and Reason: not that they thought there was no Speech without Reason; but no Reasoning without Speech.' Thomas Hobbes, *Leviathan*.

We have seen that the ideas of psychosis and God clear a space for us to examine the relation of thought to reality. In this chapter I hypothesise that speech can do the same. Hobbes points to its ability to harness reason. The suggestion is that, in tandem, reason and speech can demolish the boundaries that separate self and mind from reality. Indeed it can be said that speech leads to truth while what we hold to be feelings can lead us away from it. Sophocles has Polynices saying that the evil of exile is the loss of the freedom of speech in his home land. Polynices' mother Jocasta commented, 'Not to say what one thinks is the way of the servant.' Yet we must not forget Freud's view that ideas are hidden and need to be excavated. In other words, we do not generate ideas ourselves. They arise in conversation, and this is where speech comes in. Speech is the birth channel of ideas. Philosophy can thus be described as the release of speech. Gilbert Murray summed up what this faculty meant to the Greeks:

'The Greeks were mocked at in antiquity for being so fond of talking. It was their great glory. They believed in the power of the Logos. It was their way to settle disputes, their instrument for finding out what was true and what was fair…Traditionally [the Logos] is translated as "word"; but it is 'talk' or 'speech': sermo rather than verbum. It is the most characteristic word in the Greek language.'(1)

But what, we might ask, is there about speech that enables it to create a space for the generation of ideas? Three responses come to mind. Firstly, speech removes the need to act out our repressed impulses. Maurice Blanchot contends that: '…it transgresses laws, breaks away from orientation, it disorients.' (2) Existentialism famously exhorts us to act, but Freud suspected that acting out arises from the bundle of repressed memories, thoughts and feelings we call the unconscious. In other words, action does not imply agency. But we can say that, to an extent, speech confers agency by emptying the mind of that which blocks conscious deliberation. Secondly, speech creates a space for the generation of ideas where attention can be given to 'that' questions rather than 'what' questions. The first type of question accepts reality as bedrock; the second queries it and tries to square it with prevailing narratives. Choices (what?) and decisions (which?) are responses we make to a world we perceive as fractured. They are illusions: once made, they deny all other options. Thirdly, when we speak we leave our problems behind and let reality take up the reins. The process of speaking means we are no longer exposed to the temptation to chase after certainty, the temptation to anchor or glue together the fragments that have been created by our very perceptions in the first place.

And yet, given that actual speech so often falls beneath Hobbes' claim, we might justifiably refuse to see it as the avatar of the human. Complaints are rife today about the diminishing space available for public discussion of grand ideas. Thinking is said to have turned inward to a personal world filled with negative views, wants and needs, and loneliness. When released into the public arena this thinking nurtures a culture of complaint. At the same time, we often find that conversation is shoehorned into an uncomfortably tight space: we are invited to speak and yet, when we respond, we are quickly closed down with the comment that what we say does not fit the current narrative. Newton's law applies – there is an equal and opposite reaction for every force. And, even when some force gets through, we must navigate a labyrinth of rules delineating what can and can't be said.

People's actual speech generally fails to reveal essence. It is oppressed by fear of where it might go, of which moral prohibition it might encounter. Speech does not correlate with one's own thought or that of others, or even 'the topic' in a formal discussion, and it is not circumscribed by the ways we use language. We are generally programmed into the use of platitudes that confine speech to recounting memory and honouring custom. It doesn't matter that speech is apostrophised by swearing, insults, blasphemy, mockery, or attacks on all manner of sacred cows. The point is that it is only when we speak that philosophy reveals itself as the love of wisdom. Freedom of speech (Greek: parrhesia) is to speak truth with candour. Foucault extends it to mean speaking truth to power. But when John tells us that 'In the beginning was the Word' he is speaking metaphysically. He is saying that speech is nothing less than the search for truth and reality. Speech is more than what we feel; it is our in-the-world-ness expressing itself.

The problems we encounter with speech are in speech itself. They are not caused by the effect on speech of something extraneous to it. The process of speech is impatient for movement. And of course, subjects are notoriously preoccupied with themselves. So the gap between the person and a space for free speech widens. Nonetheless, the inhibitions we encounter are largely produced by language. Our desire to make sense of things has a flip-side. A move towards order entails the creation of propositional or logical statements. These statements break things down into rights and wrongs so that we can manage conflict. Indeed so much of what constitutes conversation is merely an exercise in sorting the goodies out from the baddies. Propositions are the holding on to a divide; we try to keep the weight from falling to either side for fear of how the 'losing' half will react. Ironically propositions are an attempt to avoid the mercurial shifts exhibited by feelings that erupt quickly and change subtly. Feelings reflect values embedded in an inner, unspoken world. They are what we do not want to give up and yet, it must be said, they take us nearer to the whole of reality than logic does. It can be argued that propositional logic fails to recognise that feelings are amorphous and pervasive. If we spoke our feelings, it can be argued further, we would get the best of all possible worlds.

Thought is another matter. In the form of opinion it works its way into discussions and, in contrast to feelings, it is more brutal in rejecting and consigning issues into the void. But Freud tells us that neurosis arises when we get in touch with ambivalence. It is tautological to point out that to choose one side of a binary divide over the other leaves out half of reality. A move towards totality requires that we integrate the absent 'dark side.' This is the 'what' issue. What then is the 'how'? How do we release flow or currents of speech so that they include the in-between? In other words, how do we have our cake and eat it? Two things are crucial here. One is process, which carries us to feelings or logic but, more important, can also embrace both. The other is thought, which depicts reality better than either feelings or logic.

And yet we hold back. The world may be full of the most mellifluous poets, but if they do not let others hear their words they are 'mute Miltons.' Speech is commonly condemned to be silent, presumably because we dread exposing ourselves to censure. Indeed speech is deemed problematic, whereas writing is not. Speech is allowed to manifest only in forms other than its own, for example as that which underlies writing. What passes for speech is almost always an avoidance of it. It occurs subversively, surreptitiously and most frankly only in anger or madness.

Otherwise it is sublimated, structured or standardised and accepted only from the mouths of children or characters in a story. We quickly ask who is speaking to whom and thereby bring the weight of social classification down on the spoken word. Speech has the power to reveal all that is concealed in speaker and listener, and yet a good case can be made for saying that people do not talk. In a world committed to the concealment of our deepest impulses it is a matter of wonder that speech emerges at all. It is not too outrageous to suppose that all speech is biased. Hearing must be put on the table alongside speaking if this process is to be opened up. That is to say, what is needed is a form of hearing that can discern the truth that lies behind attempts to polish, sift or calibrate speech. I do not mean our ears are closed to all input, although, in the postmodern world, scientific and cultural rhetoric tends to have an easy passage. But the world at large seems to comprise myriad echo chambers where anodyne and inoffensive relationships are played out. And yet, without disturbance, nothing gets through! Philosophy assumes there is among people a widespread and desperate need to be heard. Socrates put active listening forward as the only form of doing that bypasses content and elicits process. Thus listening draws out speech.

When it is only a matter of content or language, speech is usually harnessed for social purposes like the chatter that hides loneliness. Freud identified stream of consciousness as a way of overcoming psychological defences in order to reveal childhood traumas. Lacan says the arrival of language is the arrival of the superego. But this move seeks to split the psyche and to stop the id being accepted as the psyche. In any case, merely speaking about something amounts only to the conveying of content, ideology, ethics or a narrative. Philosophically, these usages equate with appearance. But speech is more than this; it gives birth to ideas. When Socrates' muse Diotima spoke to him she inspired him to speak to greater effect. The point is that we are able to think only when we speak. Only then does a thing emerge into consciousness. Speech is more fundamental than language in that it can free those who have become sunk in language.

In mythos subjectivity amounted to little more than what characters in poems were made to think or do. But the Greek Agora changed all that. A speaker was now released from the grip of custom and domesticity. People entered the Agora (and conversation) not physically but as an idea. Whereas action was previously the pinnacle of the human, inspiration now entered human relations. A self could no longer get away with using a conversation as a site of combat or argument. It dawned on people that it is not other people who frighten them. Rather it is speech, because the chief fear is that speech will bring into the light what is hidden. Speech exposes what the mind clings to.

It does this because people partake in speech. They speak not only to each other but to speech itself. The Greeks looked at ideas as hypotheses that anticipated the appearance of humankind. Thus, when humanity expresses itself through such grand ideas as love, goodness and truth, it partakes in an hypothesis. As an idea opens up it reveals more about itself and the speaker. In other words, speech is not a means to an end but an end in itself. It generates a person. Only when we speak to someone do both of us exist. In this sense, speaking is an act of love. We fall into speech in the same way we fall in love with love. As we speak we inspire ourselves not merely to convey ideas but to bring new ones to term.

Nonetheless, fresh speech will only respond to a welcome, not to a rebuff. It is too innocent to fight for the dwindling space in a mind already full of nostrums. So, to start with, we have veritably to vomit out 'our own story,' because it fills our mind to capacity. The act of vomiting acknowledges how embedded are our own narratives. We are not free while we retain our story; 'our' being the wrong attribution, for it is implanted by our parents. Only a relatively empty mind can explore the gap between speech and our self. But what is frequently misunderstood and misused is an appreciation that speech is an act of love. It rescues people from a persistent urge to become a spectacle or celebrity, or to treat life as an aesthetic exercise. Spectacle, celebrity and aestheticism are diversions that enable people to hold on to notions of body and mind and perpetuate a sense of self. So we must find an anchor outside the self if we are barely to exist.

The final move is from speech to conversation (con-verse is to speak together). The process that underpins a conversation is the continuity between what each speaker says. There is something in a conversation that unfolds as it draws in each individual. It is not destroyed by silences or interjections of feeling or opinion. What is revealed is the relation of speaking to listening. Socrates' role in the dialogues makes clear that it is not what was said to him that determined what he heard but his ability to listen. The contrary view to Socrates' is offered by evolution theory. It says we are programmed to accept that which adds to our capacity to survive and reject that which doesn't. This can merely amount to finding friends and detaching from enemies. It is saying no more than that we should fight back against whatever is said that threatens our preconceived views. Connection in this sense is a dubious process.

In order to stimulate frank exchanges Socrates took upon himself the task of evoking speech in his interlocutors. He was a midwife at the birth of speech because he associated it with the search for truth. It reconciles not just the opposites of subject and object but also those of imagination and reason. Its opposite is not non-speech (mute) but the application of speech to the service of anything other than truth. Speech is not, as Wittgenstein suggests, a choice between silence and language: it incorporates both. To oppose speech to the written word a la Derrida is to mistake them both. The written word is speech because both are ways of leaving the self behind and entering the world. Socrates realised that the listener is the fulcrum of conversation, or more pertinently that it is the quality of listening that matters, not the speaker. Socrates spoke as the audience to his friends; he was a kind of Greek chorus that cajoled, provoked, questioned and inspired the actors. He helped give birth to speech in others by offering himself as the attentive, non-judgemental listener they'd always craved.

Socrates personified speech as a search for truth and reality. The search is an act of courage because the moment we engage openly and frankly with another person we enter the unknown. Socrates warned us we would never acquire total knowledge of others. In any case, truth and reality are not products of knowledge. Indeed, engagement with another requires that we let go of rules and obligations. Yet we do know something. We know that matters proceed afoot when we accept that we *know* something about another person, rather than we know *something* about them. The emphasis is on the object, not the subject; indeed, the object initially becomes the fulcrum. Needless to say, a subject believes it is real or a self. It possesses a body like any other animal, but the body amounts only to a temporary arrest of ideation. Classical philosophy says that the world is made up of ideas in which I, the subject, am also an idea. An idealist would say the subject also dies, that it is only a linguistic illusion. But classical philosophy takes another tack. It releases process by evolving preparatory ideas to wake us up to grander ones. Thus it reveals the world to be a cornucopia of ideas at different stages of gestation.

CHAPTER THIRTEEN: THE HUMAN EMERGES IN FRIENDSHIP

'[Friendship] alone, of all the loves, seemed to raise you to the level of gods or angels.' CS Lewis, *The Four Loves*.

I have argued that speech transforms the space between people into an engine of ideas. It forces thought to engage with reality. Now we can see where friendship finds a role. It is a space in which these developments unfold. Plato acclaimed friendship as one of the highest virtues: it is the point on which all expressions of love converge in a search for truth. Friendship is nothing less than the underpinning of life; it opens our minds and hearts to reality. Philia is a Greek term for strong feelings for a particular other. Agape is more demanding. It means to possess a heart strong enough to handle the fullest engagement with anyone who comes across our path. The Greeks opposed it to erotic coupledom, which largely revolves around sexual exclusivity (to which I chiefly attribute the failure of the family in an earlier chapter). Agape conveys much more than Aristotle's 'perfect' friendship. Perfect friendship survives even when the ostensible reasons that brought the couple together come to an end – for example, conversations with an hairdresser end when one moves to another hairdresser. But Platonic agape or friendship points to a meta-position standing above and beyond the intimacy of the friends. This position allows for differences in the friendship to emerge without the whole collapsing. This is an exemplification of the in-between, second only to the Agora. It grants ontological status to friendship.

Thus the Greek version of friendship goes far beyond chats over coffee and getting up-to-date with someone. That particular arrangement savours of two selves coming together; it remains in the realm of appearance. Indeed, despite the distress caused by the subjectivity-laden identity culture of recent times, subjectivity reigns supreme in philosophy and in culture at large. The Kantian Catastrophe killed off the noumena or the object, leaving philosophy ill-disposed to otherness or objectivity. But subjectivity only tolerates extensions of itself. In effect it is an echo chamber. So, in the absence of objectivity, subjectivity needs something else to pitch itself against. An encounter with others is the only candidate. An encounter might throw us into the fiery cauldron of a large interactive group, community or a gathering like the Agora. There we will have to respond to a challenge to accept everyone as a friend - agape - which I will deal with in the next chapter. Or it might develop into a relationship between two, which I deal with here. I do not mean the intensity of attraction of philia, which can come close to the bonding that characterises erotic attraction. I follow the Greek invitation to a friendship that is not held together by an addictive passion.

The Greeks understood friendship as essence and society as appearance. Friends abide in the realm of the interpersonal, noumena and love. Society lies in the realm of phenomena, custom, habit, obligation and network.

Friendship is so rich in human succour compared to society that it behoves us to ask if we have been duped into believing that social networks can provide the enrichment they promise. Albeit we can take it that (over time) the phenomenon of society casts its shadow over the essence of friendship. This is not to say that everyone colludes with society. A minority has always seen through the promises of class, nation and kibbutz. All the same, 'Man is born free but he is everywhere in chains,' as Rousseau reminds us.

Everyone desires things to be personal, warm and close-knit, or so they say. Yet, on closer examination, it can be seen that the way we actually engage with friends and partners, however generous our intentions, amounts to little more than rehearsals from a repertoire of gestures, smiles, breezy non-sequiturs, and practised responses that do scant justice to friendship. And so, when we are asked to raise the bar and discuss the very idea of relating, things fall apart. Leibowitz courageously steps forward and says we simply cannot relate to one another anyway, unless we do it through God. And even then, with God as a mediator, we are only capable of relating to each other as members of a community. The question: What forestalls us? remains open. Is it that we sense something inside ourselves that overawes us when a more reflective approach to friendship is on offer, or is it that the discussion itself overawes us?

The Greeks already understood the Freudian contention that we will suffer mental ill-health if we don't separate from parents and siblings. They recognised that detachment from others is more important than attachment, that we cannot move from connection by association to true connection (community) until we are prepared to make this first move. Interestingly, present-day society encourages more attachment and closer association. Alain Badiou writes of the move of two subjectivities towards the larger subjectivity of Love. (1) They never leave subjectivity behind. Yet against this view it can be said that our ability to relate in later life increases the earlier we make this break. Until we and our potential friends are free of the clinging, negative influence of others, we will not be capable of sustaining a close, one-to-one relationship. It follows that the building of a wall around two lovers or friends can only work when they each already possess a personal boundary. They each need a slate wiped clean of prior attachments. But people struggle to acquire an uncontaminated relation to others. They try to release themselves from enmeshment with parents or siblings by erecting in their own minds a boundary against nearest and dearest. But the power of this internal boundary is tenacious. It can't be reduced in later life simply by getting close to someone else. An attempt to put a boundary around two lovers or friends who have not already individuated is doomed to failure.

The Greeks learned a valuable lesson about friendship from their dissatisfaction with the One and Many issue. One and Many were treated as two sides of a dichotomy that refused to connect. But aggregation offers a better alternative to dichotomised thinking. Aggregation tells us that opposites are not mutually exclusive. It makes allowance for non-logical relationships between opposites such that they can lead either to union between the opposites or to the appearance of a meta-concept that embraces both sides of the divide. The idea of aggregation is directly applicable to human relations. Two people are no longer forced to form One out of the fusion of two. Nor need the pair struggle to preserve their independence as distinct entities by keeping each other at arms' length. Friendship abhors the dance of opposites that is the modern version of the dialectic. It produces an excess that needs to be handled further down the road. The Greeks would have seen this version of the dialectic as the greatest enemy of movement because it only allows a shift from one solid position to another. Such an event will thus hold all movement within itself. The Greeks sought a relationship which combined independence and intimacy. This they found occurs only under the umbrella of the meta idea of friendship. As CS Lewis points out, friendship is 'the least natural of loves; the least instinctive, organic, biological, gregarious and necessary.' Eros is usually necessary for begetting, and affection is usually part of child-rearing. But we can live and breed without friendship. Moreover two friends will abstain from nerve-jangling outbursts; they have drawn apart from the world and entered 'in that luminous, tranquil, rational world of relationship freely chosen.' (2) This move explains why the nexus of parents and child, which Freud adduced as the centre of human relating, fails to help the child move forward and form mature adult relationships. A couple who treat their love bond as all-important have chosen fusion over friendship. The child comes second. The Greeks sought a form of adult intimacy that did not collapse into fusion. A love potion merely supplies a rickety foundation for the romance of family.

The Greeks made a breakthrough when they realised that it takes more than the discovery of another person to form a relationship. True connection requires the two parts to relate through the whole. Leibowitz and Levinas are better guides than Freud in this matter. Leibowitz places God as the third in the relationship; Levinas introduces the 'alterity' of the other alongside their bodily presence. It may seem cold-hearted or impersonal to shift the focus of a relationship away from the two ostensible protagonists. But it would be better to broaden our perception and see this move as reflecting an impersonal aspect of the personal. The relationship now assumes the status of a meta-idea filled with possibilities that are absent in face-face meetings between actual people. By depicting a relationship as two parts connecting through the whole the Greeks did something extraordinary. Socrates realised that the deep wounds in the other (friend or partner) would never be healed by direct connection. Too much was unexplored in this way, too much left unsaid.

Psychology draws on Greek myths and philosophical insights to explain the Greek celebration of friendship. It says there are two key moves in life. The first is attachment. This term sounds positive. Nonetheless it can be predatory. It rebounds on us when we focus on the baby's love for the mother. Society endorses this move. Yet the persistence of this memory is not to do with love; it is fear of the loss of attachment. The second move is detachment. Its importance cannot be underestimated. Without it we cannot proceed to the conceptualising of things. Philosophy is dedicated to the completion of this move. Unless we detach from our initial primary carer, we will seek to possess our friend or partner. Possession is not love. Only when we detach from the oneness that characterises the bond with our mother will we be able to create two distinct entities. Only now can the highest form of connection be made with the world - between two independent entities. And ironically, when we free our friend or partner from our possessive grasp, we free ourselves. This is where philosophy comes in. This freedom allows a profound sense of love to emerge. In other words, relationships have a basis in loss, a basis that opens us up to risk-taking. It they are integral to the search for truth; they are our entry into the world. To biologise or concretise connection is to lose all sight of its potential. When we settle for the physical aspects of the other we neglect the role of the mind in the relationship. When we fail to conceptualise the relationship we lose our connection to the muse, to divinity, sublimity and inspiration. We turn to action for its own sake. To settle for less is to submit to society's imperatives. These ask us to operate only at the level of rituals like birthdays and other ceremonies, and roles like mother and father.

Relationship means 'to know the other' in the Bible, But this kind of knowing requires us to let go of the self. We must ask: What is this edifice of self we seek to preserve? The self is an amalgam of all the people (their manners, opinions and world views) who have influenced us, whom we respected or felt accepted by. And where did they gain these attributes but ultimately from society – the media, films, books and so on? The self is not given to us personally. So ironically, the more we drop our guard and let the other in, the more we come to accept our place in the universe. Even then, relationships can take years to flourish because they are emergent processes. Much as we might protest to the opposite, they are not determined by personal attraction, preference or individual qualities either. These determinants arise from a subjective stance. Yet subjects project themselves onto others instead of trying to understand them. No, a relationship is the fulcrum itself. It emerges when we no longer take ourselves as the fulcrum, when we stop being concerned with our own preferences.

Friendship is an idea, not a human disposition. Its application in life involves a persistent coming up to the line, whatever the disappointments or rebuffs experienced. Relationships can be said to be a replacement for otherness. Levinas' otherness is in danger of emerging as just another subjective projection. It might become merely the relation between two beings who project their subjectivity onto each other and offer mutual support in a crisis. Based on an obligation to offer help, it fails to create space for the emergence of a relationship that has the power to annihilate the self.

But how can we know friendship? We must first stop trying to know about friendship. The 'about' question implies a detachment from the friendship. We then contemplate friendship rather than engage with it. To know a connection is to connect to the connection itself. The 'about' question seeks an answer that is amenable to knowledge. Ironically it can only arise from a human who wants to keep a relationship at arm's length. So to know a relationship is to recognise we are part of what we observe. What then does this mean when, for example, we first come face to face with a person? Of course, our first response might be to reach for a manual of social rules of engagement. But this will fail to incorporate the observer into reality. This approach takes for granted that what is happening between people is played out in the mind of the observer. There, the 'inside' has been allowed to intrude into the process of observing. Out of this process feelings arise in the observer that intimidate and confuse because they carry such dynamism, such energy - and such social censure. There is a danger that it is these feelings and not the other person or object to which one relates. Leibowitz takes us further. Agreeing that the essence of humanity is the interpersonal or communal, he nonetheless requires that the other be added. Only then can we turn to God and see what it means to stand shoulder to shoulder with another human. Everything else is an idol. In other words, we can only turn to the other via God. Neither the 'I' nor the other is the carrier of truth. The other is necessary for us to discover the truth, but it can be an obstacle too if we ignore the idea that lies behind it.

As presently constituted, philosophy discusses at best half of what pertains to the human. The problem is that the unit chosen has always been the person. To go beyond this point has been deemed to go beyond the reach of philosophy. The bugbear is consciousness. It is an unsatisfactory concept for it is assumed to reside inside the skull. And yet animation cannot be confined to the domain of the self. This move can't explain the free-ranging movement of feelings. Freud was wrong to trace all things human to individual consciousness. Pan-consciousness has a much better claim. Our present best efforts must be directed to mapping the territory of relationships and shared feelings. Only then can we appreciate that my loving you is you loving me. Love is now ontological. The 'it' of love (instead of its application: love of or for someone) does not lie in the domain of subject or object. It follows that any behaviour emanating from a person does not originate from them. It is a reaction to the feelings of other people.

A friendship is a case in point. It is the phoenix that arises from the death of self. The claim to be an 'I' is a second move. Our origin is outside the Cave. But when we start a sentence with 'I' we are in the Cave. The question to ask is not: how do I climb out? But: how did I end up here? Could it be that I couldn't face the horror of being? Heidegger blames consciousness for offering us a glimpse of this earlier world before consciousness then fragments it into small particulars. Our response up to this point has been to let our soul fall into the embrace of erotic love and attachment. Socrates offered to remove the ties that bind our thoughts to erroneous solutions. But his move did not refill the mind with new energy or impulse. We must move deeper into philosophy for this to happen. The danger is that we will respond to the song of the sirens and turn back. And the most insidious of these songs tells us that our nearest and dearest are still in the Cave and will feel lost if we move on. The backward glance has long been seen to foretell doom. The Greek god Orpheus looks back towards Hades and thus loses his wife Eurydice; in the Bible Lot's wife looks back to Sodom and is turned into a pillar of salt. We give our freedom away so lightly; survivors' guilt weighs heavily.

People relate more than they are prepared to acknowledge. When we take up a position outside Plato's Cave we can see that feelings do not belong to a person but reside in them only temporarily. By choosing wellness as a default position we can address the retreat into the Cave. I am aware this means that this book is not offering to be a helpmeet in the sense of holding someone's hand and guiding them out of the Cave. We start outside the Cave from the outset because people have to become aware that there is already something profound in them, something that yet lies dormant. It hovers outside the ethical prison they believe they still share with parents or siblings. Philosophy is a reminder of a period before we turned to charity for help, a period when we were sustained by connections in the form of love, friendship and community. This something knows we are free and that we do not need to atone for our freedom. The analogy of Plato's Cave tells us that earlier, dark moments in human history were only transient crises, that we are free once we address whatever still draws us back to those times. We can stop converting the social indoctrination we've received into personal pain. A turn to philosophy opens up alternatives to stale thought. For example, Heidegger laments the divorce of thinking and experience from being. He points to what happens when we start to cast doubt on feelings and experiences. He points to something much grander that lies dormant in us.

Appearance is the culprit. We enter a world of guilt and remorse when we rely on feelings and experiences. To try and gain an understanding of things beyond experience we must nurture the soul of community (without resort to fascism, mob rule or crowd psychology). When we succumb to experience we prepare the ground for society. People enmeshed in a clinging relationship are likely to locate the trouble in their partner. They rarely locate it in relationship qua relationship. We say we are either too close or too remote and then withdraw. But why not go further, not to the other, but to a deeper understanding of friendship itself? The counterpoint to appearance is essence; the counterpoint to the individual is connection. Essence, as Deleuze and Guattari point out, is psychotic; it follows no clear path, assumes no clear form. So, let us not pin connection down.

Beyond ontology is is-ness and is-ness is passion or yearning. We can for the moment call it reality plus what reality hides. What is hidden is that which passes between people. It can be said that we already have everything in common with each other but our response to this commonality differs. Our first move is a passionate response to others. David Smail believes that clinical psychology fails people when it identifies a problem in the individual (even if it promises to resolve this problem). Relational, interpersonal and systemic forces (the in-between) far outweigh those within a person. (3) Only relationships introduce reality into life. When a passionate response passes between people Nietzsche's Dionysus begins to emerge. But a second move occurs when reason responds to passion. This is Nietzsche's Apollo. Plato puts reason (Apollo) above feelings (Dionysus), Freud almost so. Reason attempts to do something about the stimulus of passion. Passion itself derives from the body, the lower brain; it is mostly triggered by the interpersonal, by relationship. This is what needs releasing.

How then can we relate more felicitously? Firstly, we don't need to focus on the faults of the other. Rather, we can ask if we know the other well enough. To question one's responses to the other is to challenge the self's attempt to control the world. If we see only faults in them we've succumbed to appearance, because ontology is not fractured into fault lines. We will see faults when we sink into a sense of self. So, empty yourself of all me-me demands and let the other take centre stage. The question then arises: What do I do with no-me, a sense that I am not here? One answer is to give it full validation by neither dominating the other (being their parent) nor running away from them (fearing them as the parent).

Secondly, we must challenge the human predilection to care for others more than for oneself. We so easily believe we let down our nearest and dearest. We refuse to hold our heads high and free our lives to fly where they will for fear these moves will be at the expense of others. We can now reverse the process because - irony of ironies - we did not let them down at all early enough! Until a child can face the rigours of the world it will not handle adulthood. (It goes without saying I do not mean gross neglect or violence.) Prolonged protection from the emotional slings and arrows of the world weakens our power of resilience. We will survive and flourish, nonetheless. In fact, until we do this we will not relate, for we will look to the other as a protector or surrogate parent. This is not an argument for neglect but a plea for inaction (non-meddling) in the life of our partner.

Philosophy invites us to be the audience in the world. It suggests we observe life rather than live it. It enjoins us to give up wishing to be a part of the spectacle. A parent invites a child to live in the world, not to be subsumed in it. Ethics is an attempt to prevent successful detachment. So, observe and do not become involved! Acknowledge that the world needs witnessing. Otherwise, the world will become swamped by phenomena.

Thirdly, we need not worry about losing a protective boundary between us and the other. The in-between is already the boundary. The in-between is reality. We don't need society to tell us to batten down or sublimate strong feelings. The self is already doing its best to give shape and direction to what happens between people. Society and the zeitgeist will step in to structure or domesticate reality when the self fails. The in-between is ontological. If we fail to recognise this, we will feel forced to make a superfluous response to it. We would have done better to leave well alone, to let reality take its course. Our attempts to deal with feelings and connection make us emerge as individuals. But this is not itself human essence. It is a response to it.

Socrates encouraged us to expand his vision of friendship into a community of enquirers. These friends will love, not the 'I' or the other, because these are only stepping-stones, but wholeness and truth that lie beyond them. This vision manifests in the Agora.

CHAPTER FOURTEEN: THE HUMAN EMERGES IN THE AGORA

'At least you can sense that they philosophised differently in Athens, above all in public. Nothing is less Greek than the conceptual cobwebbery of a hermit.' Friedrich Nietzsche, *Twilight of the Idols*.

The crowning glory of all previous moves was entry to the Agora. I stress at the outset that the Agora is a vision of Socrates that underpins all the dialogues. Here Socrates intended to build a de-politicised society out of the prevailing non-society. Despite the fact that Greek politics was the very model of a direct democracy it was still politics. It responded to the two forces of the self and the socio. Socrates wanted to introduce an idea that took society beyond the mere trading of factional wants, defences and phobias; beyond the negotiating of an uneasy balance between tyranny and mob rule. The compromises that then ensue degrade and imprison the human spirit. People become defeatist in the face of a politics that only offers a way of living within self-imposed limitations. They start to accept that things will always be the way they presently are. Their lives are determined by how far they climb the greasy pole of aspiration, itself constructed from values that underpin politics. He wanted individuals to be confident enough in themselves for them to talk, interact and create an enlivening process at the crux of which is human relating.

The Agora is where all the seemingly incongruent forces of reason, emotionality, and group process are let loose. In the resulting melee the deeper congruence of all things is revealed. This grounds the participants in reality. Minds that have become alienated from the world are now forced to address their own aberrations in the same way a furnace burns away impurities to reveal pure metal. If Socrates was concerned pre-eminently with any one thing it was individuation. He was convinced that two humans can only connect when each is completely individuated. People offer their differences, warts and all to each other. To do this they must be able to stand entirely apart from society. Ironically, connection occurs through difference. As Deleuze put it, the difference between the couple is revealed as a matter of intensity. On the other hand, society strives to make connections by devising artifices such as identity or role, which only keep connection at arm's length. Freud's ideas reflect a social fear that the release of the id from the prison of the superego will lead to murder, rape and mayhem. As Chapter Eight pointed out, this fear merely serves to nurture the socio.

We may never know the source of Socrates' inspiration, but we know that his concern for the god-likeness of humans drew him unerringly to what happens when they assemble. Socrates' intuited that the essence of humanity lay here. But this was not just any form of assembly. So much in ancient Greece revolved around its democracy. But Socrates looked far beyond the question of political freedom and human governance to the universal questions of reality and truth. The apogee of his vision was a philosophical free-for-all in the Agora. The Greek term Aga signifies greatness. We've already come across Agape, which means possessing a heart big enough to love everyone. The Agora is the great open space at the centre of the city on which everyone converges to speak, entertain, worship, do business, or philosophise. It is the heart of the city. When humans participate in a no-holds-barred, intellectual encounter, Socrates is telling us, narcissism loses its power to obstruct the search for truth. A citizen's thoughts can range across the whole landscape when they are not trapped in a neurotic, private realm. They can move freely within reality, for the Agora is the world. Everyone finds a place, for the Agora is grand enough to embrace all citizens, warts and all. There is no need for people to contort themselves to fit into a one-size-fits-all system. The Agora is the parent who encourages the child to be themselves, to individuate and not worry about the preservation of family ethos or image. It is the site of free speech and friendship beyond the pressures of demagogy, persuasion or the attraction of the mass. The carapace of self is burned away as idols are challenged. The individuated human learns what it means to be psychotic as the Agora's cauldron-heat produces an intimate intermingling and a fiery challenge to norms.

Socrates looked to this enlivening assembly to provide the foundations of a new society. His model of Athenian citizenship required an aspirant's mind to be free of the self-protecting, guarded and introverted mind-frame he associated with families in general. Citizenship required that the negative thoughts people have about themselves be emptied and not channelled into causes. Good works and charitable campaigns channel energy towards the good and away from truth. His sense of citizenship demanded more than the offloading of one's worries and prejudices in the public concourse. Something has to happen before young men entered the polis on the principle that the loves, hates, confusions and prejudices with which the mind is awash would otherwise make political life impossible. In Socrates' time Greek democracy was direct; free speech was guaranteed; everyone could speak and vote in the Assembly. No special powers were given to wealth. But, as the example of Socrates shows, it was impossible to avoid offending others. The problem for such a democracy was its openness to sophism, rhetoric and rumour. Liberty had opened the door to the tyranny of populism and mass persuasion. Socrates argued that a well-ordered state needed, not just citizens who are free to speak, but citizens who carried no resentments or inner conflicts and accordingly could resist the pressure of others to think in given ways. When they spoke it was to be from an unprejudiced and fearless mind. This is the object of a Socratic interrogation. An encounter with Socrates flushed one's mind clear of its contents, fears and phobias. Such an aspirant would then be ready to enter the final stage of philosophical development - public participation in the Agora – prior to becoming a legislator or administrator.

The Agora was a Socratic vision. Plato accepted it at first but went off it in later life. He always had low expectations of 'the mad Athenian demos' (1) and probably never forgave Greek democracy for killing Socrates. But it must be stressed that the Agora was of a different order to democracy, even the demanding versions found in Greece. The Agora's special form of direct relating never lost its intensity and never ended; it made politics redundant. It treated each citizen as a complete polity in themselves, able to handle their own inner assembly of conflicting interests. They could already deal with the basic issues of living with themselves and others. They could thus carry the meaning of society to another level without the leavening of politics. Today it is often said that everything is political, even family relationships, work or love. This may apply if we take ourselves forever to be what we were before a Socratic dialogue. But the world is different after a meeting with Socrates. One can now conceive of the Agora as a de-politicised zone. The nostrum that politics is the art of the possible, of compromise, no longer limits our thinking. This merely means that ethics and the idea of goodness go unchallenged. But truth and reality are the lodestars for the Agora.

Socrates wanted to raise the Greeks' game. He believed that their superiority over surrounding tribes hid some serious flaws in their thinking. They were resting on their laurels. Of course, ideas are always in danger of ossifying, and it was to shake them up in daily acts of dishevelment that the Agora found its function. Encounters there would be like being bitten by a cloud of gadflies. Minor issues dropped away. It brought human aggregation and the ideas of unity and reality together to profound effect. Whereas Socratic dialogues tend to follow agreed rules of engagement, (2) the Agora released primal forces that broke down the barriers between people, between ideas, and between people and ideas. The resulting combustion would create numerous aporias . All the dots that minds had separated could be joined up again. No stone was left unturned in the search for truth and reality. The Agora spirit maintained that everything can be philosophised. It promised to reveal for example that an unexamined metaphysical question lies behind the most intractable of personal feuds, and that emotional eruptions can be understood as an integral feature of heightened group process. These events are not failures of relationship so much as opportunities to explore further. Now, when a person stumbles for words, is inflamed by the words of another, or stands against the general flow, the group sets process in motion again by putting the incident or hiatus into the most general context. Monism is restored.

Speech is to be encouraged without limit; psychosis to transgress the barriers set up by neurosis; idols are toppled at will; ideas are manufactured in bursts of exuberance; and friendships blossom and joyfully overstep the bounds of polite society. Saliency loses its meaning as the difference between foreground and background vanishes. Totality become the only reference point; no particular thing is privileged to the extent that it hinders the appearance of other things. There are no parts, only All. Nothing is identified, unless there is a willingness to embrace the totality of identities. Tension builds as diehard opinions fracture under interrogation. Purpose, meaning and certainties crumble in long moments of stark clarity. Nothing is there for its own sake, only to facilitate the emergence of more ideas. Aporia offers glimpses of truth as the walls of moral disapprobation crack open. When hiatuses interrupt the general flow of conversation, it becomes the task of 'process' people in the gathering to release the flow again. They step in to facilitate when feelings run high, oppositions arise, or misunderstandings obscure the reality trawled up by process. Contributors are able to rise above squabbles because they have dispensed with a sense of self. Socrates is the role model.

The Agora was a state of mind. The key requirement was to turn up, not to catch the eye by saying something clever. The ability of the process to handle anything that arose was taken for granted. Upsets revealed reality. Topics arose from the initial coming-together of people;

they had a natural life span and blossomed and died. Nothing was prearranged. Accordingly nothing was seen as a problem to be solved. No distinction was made between feelings and philosophy because human life was taken to be the starting point of both. Everything was seen as an extension of everything else. Socratic philosophy wanted nothing more than to release process - the movement and interaction of all things. The Agora was a vision of such an encounter. It proclaimed: there is only otherness, so submit to it. You have nothing in you to defend.

A large (37 acres) physical space was preserved in central Athens where men over 18 years of age were allowed to gather. (3) Socrates envisaged this space being filled with a melee of conversations that would generate concepts out of the materials and struggles in their lives. Nothing would faze the conversationalists. Consciousness would no longer be a burden that needs to be handled. Instead, the human capacity to think would flourish in an exploration of everything. A verbal, all-rules-barred, free-for-all encounter would open the door to human liberty. Socrates did not intent to take us anywhere but to open up the space hidden by the self. The culprit was the mind, whether in itself or its effect. The Greeks worked out that the mind's tendency to turn inward was not preordained. Society had of course stepped forward as a valid attempt to prevent people from sinking deep into themselves. Everyone could now think about social issues. At one stroke the problem of the individual mind was solved. But society immediately muddied the water. Instead of building on this mental redirection, it turned the mind into a problem in and of itself. The projection of the self into society had only produced a situation in which minds engaged with other minds in a closed loop. Aggregation had produced replication. Everything was homogenised; no new thoughts were admitted. The lack of challenge to certainties bred a belief in the efficacy of law. In the end, all that society had done was to prevent each mind from engaging with otherness, with fundamental difference, which is the doorway to reality.

Profoundly aware of these problems, Socrates set out to redesign the way we live. The idea of the Agora took shape. Two obstacles to truth had to be removed at the outset. They arose from the predilection of the 'I' to talk to others about itself and to expect others to talk about the 'I'/ 'me.' So the first obstacle was the 'I'/ 'me.' Can we, Socrates asked, bring about the suicide of the self? The second problem was the other, a key issue that we post-moderns fail to address. Can we, he asked, commit the homicide of the other? Can we stop clinging to those whom we perceive to be a source of pleasure, help or encouragement? They offer short-term sustenance, but in the long-term they only offer the prospect of habit-forming stasis and, finally, an end to the search for truth. Fascination with self and other people has turned our lives into the worship of sacred cows. Nothing now matters but intimacy, erotic love, image, habit, domesticity, work and division of labour. As a result, minds overflow with fears, anxieties, prejudices, loyalties and preoccupations. The modern aim to maximise personal happiness has merely burnished the image of the self. The Greeks had a grander aim: the creation of a free citizenry. This required a physical and psychic space where all citizens-to-be flushed out of their minds the strategies that nurtured the self. Left to itself the mind had dehumanised humans! In other words, the Agora would replace both society and self as the site of human development. Only in this way would humanity's problems be solved. A community of friends will reach out beyond family, clan, identity and social classifications to the strangers on the margins of their lives. Unlimited connection was now on the cards. Today's hardening of society along lines of identity gives us a measure of the challenge.

The Agora pulled energy in two ways. Firstly: towards individuation. Socrates' intense interrogations emptied his interlocutors' minds of preconceptions. Secondly, each citizen was treated as an independent, self-governing polity. Each became the basis of the communal polity, not, as later, merely the recipient of rights handed down by the communal polity. A community of independent citizens was formed from the bottom up. In modern times, Hobbes was to foreground the community and Hegel to prioritise the state ahead of the individual citizen. But the Greek Agora celebrated the interaction between an individual and the community. For the Greeks this was a win-win situation: the two forces of individuation and community powerfully enhanced each other. This approach confounded the philosophical meaning of dichotomy. The two sides of a divide were not opposed to each other; they were both enhanced. Society treats individuals and community as opposite sides of a dichotomy, but philosophy recognises them as two aspects of an intimate relationship.

The Agora recognised society's limits. The version of human assembly offered by the Agora was not reality, but it did remove obstacles that prevent us from accessing it. It did this by stopping selves (or minds) conversing with themselves (their own minds). It brought a cacophony of different minds to bear on every single mind such that each mind had no chance of conversing with itself or adopting a social mind set. The Agora was a cauldron that burns away all clingy, equivocating and divisive mental impurities. It acts like an infernal machine of creative destruction. It carries into practise Heraclitus' claim that war is the underlying force in the world. Out of this cauldron emerged the self-less human. It demanded a commitment to the power of process to release all blockages that arise from ego, resentment and excessive feelings.

It was a metaphor for the world at large. Although it was an actual space in Athens where people congregated in order to meet friends, trade goods or conduct political inquests, it was more profoundly, a vision or idea, hinted at throughout the Socratic Dialogues. It was an idea of an encounter with human complexity in which the presence of a large number of people neutralises the fascination with another person found in one-to-one relationships. As was pointed out in the previous chapter, these latter find it difficult to counter the power of narcissism and selfhood. Encounters in the Agora could do this because they were merciless in ferreting out bombast, conformity and falsity. No heroes were lauded; no romances left unquestioned; no status deferred to. A radical energy was released. Speaking was no longer governed by the rules of domesticity. Room was created for inspiration to touch all the participants. We can understand Plato's association of the wise woman Diotima, who acted as Socrates' muse, with the profound ideas generated in the Agora. Diotima personified the Agora. Both offered themselves as a muse. Diotima related to Socrates in the same way he related to his interlocutors. Diotima and the Agora stood at the apex of a pyramid of inspiration. They produced an overflow of ideas that cascaded downwards to individual friends of Socrates and then outwards into the streets of Athens.

The Agora was the answer to the riddle of mind. Things start when curiosity leads humans into encounters with others. Immediately we realise we are no longer bystanders in the world. But involvement throws up a problem: most of us believe we have fallen under the controlling gaze of others. Resistance to this gaze seems impossible. And yet, when we start to think about it, we realise the gaze is internal. Philosophical questioning reveals that the issue is not a personal affliction but an internalisation of a split between consciousness and reality. Our minds have split in accordance with what has happened in the universe. Yet we take this move personally, as if an unconscious zone has separated from the conscious mind. We assume part of consciousness is our own and part imported from others. Imported consciousness - the gaze - controls us. This is not so much a problem when nature constituted the gaze that inhabits the unconscious. But society has replaced nature. The unconscious is now filled with social values and injunctions. We have been colonised by society and its imperatives.

The result is that we cannot convey our thoughts or hear those of others. The remedy is straightforward - reverse the gaze. A gazed-upon mind fills up with defensive thoughts that torment as they ossify. But more pertinently, a cluttered mind cannot conceptualise. The philosophical tool is out of reach. Plato tells us that conceptualisation creates reality. In other words, the perpetual emergence of the human depends on our doing something! The unblocking of the mind will allow us to share thoughts; shared thinking will once again open the mind to totality. And a mind tuned to totality can start to see the other as an object again, instead of as a projection of the subject. If this move is deferred, Plato reminds us, the appearances our mind picks up will solidify into a sense of somethingness, of false certainty, of structures, hierarchies and categories. We will have lost touch with process, indeterminacy, and human freedom. So it is imperative we speak.

But what kind of speaking? Firstly, the Agora spirit instilled a trust that one would be listened to. This was indeed the case because listeners ignored the identity or status of the speakers and paid heed only to messages conveyed beneath the words. Now the urge to broadcast one's opinions was appeased. Ad hominem remarks and demands to verify claims lost their appeal. Listeners now delved with impunity into what the words hid. Above all, the Agora showed that wonder and friendship emerge only when there are no rules or authorities. All impediments to flow or flux were put down to speech itself, not to other people. An end to roles and rules cleared the way for people of wisdom to rise to the top.

The Agora embodied the idea of the meta, the idea that embraces all fragments of wholeness. It built on the insight that separate parts of a whole can relate to each other only through the whole. As explained in the last chapter, there is always a third element in a relationship. The Agora offered itself as the third. We diminish the profundity of a relationship if we try to make it work at the level of one-to-one. Entities cannot relate without the intercession of a vibrant in-between. Intense pull-push energies generated by complexity or wholeness demand recognition and release. As they enter conversation a lightness descends. Versions of the Agora are found in Herman Hesse's Glass Bead Game and in CS Lewis's account of a heaven emptied of selfhood and possessiveness. Here is Lewis:

'They did not know the first rule of the holy game, which is that every player must by all means touch the ball and then immediately pass it on. To be found with it in your hands is a fault: to cling to it, death. But when it flies to and fro among the players too swift for the eye to follow...then indeed the eternal dance "makes heaven drowsy with the harmony."...As we draw nearer to its uncreated rhythm, pain and pleasure sink almost out of sight.' (4)

The unremitting intensity encountered in the Agora conjured up images of a clash of worlds. Differences and oppositions unravelled, likes and dislikes blurred and receded, revealing relationship of the like never encountered before. It was a category-step beyond what is usually meant by relationship. Freud tells us we are unable to relate if we have not separated from our early primary carers. Socrates understood this and made his first task the release of his interlocutors from the mores and mental habits acquired in their family of origin. The Agora took up the task from this point. A protagonist was thrown into the cauldron of an encounter amidst others in a mental and emotional helter-skelter. Participants were catapulted into full adult relationships in the Agora. Those who flunked the test might walk away from the Agora and return to domesticity, to the worship of idols, and the burnishing of a kaleidoscopic inner life. But, those who stayed would be exhilarated by the knowledge, the true knowing, of what it means creatively and fulsomely to be thrown among a motley of other citizens. The gathering was a physical incarnation of the philosophical 'third.' This is Leibowitz's God. Only now does the protagonist discern the deep profundity of the relating process. He or she has become part of what Herman Hesse called *The Glass Bead Game*, Rumi described as taking shelter among those who need no shelter, and Deleuze calls schizophrenia. We now fully enter the world as we immerse ourselves heart and soul, entering and disconnecting from fusion with others, identifying and disidentifying with all things, but never being held or fixed for long. Old ties are broken: relations with primary carers are permanently reconfigured. The effect is far-reaching. Participants might once have baulked when their partner or close friend established a bond with another friend because they wanted to keep their life compartmentalised. But now they welcome it because they have widened a friendship circle that may continue to expand indefinitely. They have helped bring more friendship into the world.

The idea of the Agora owes much to Heraclitus. He was aware that the mind is doomed to aloneness. Accordingly it seeks other minds. But then things go wrong - bifurcation occurs. In one direction we can go in search of comfort, pleasure and empathy, all of which promise to alleviate loneliness. Heidegger reminds us why: he talks of the horror of being thrown into the world. This direction offers but the most distant echo of reality. In the other direction lies philosophy. Philosophers acknowledge that the child-like, needy feelings and fragility of people drive them apart. But Heraclitus pointed to the unity of opposites. Encounters in the Agora were intended to follow Heraclitus' line and gradually bridge differences. Vibrant encounters would ensue. The Agora was a grand vision that went far beyond granting small political freedoms. What are they when we are not free in ourselves? The Agora made it patently clear that society doesn't emerge from the mere tinkering with the mechanisms of governance in the hope that better compromises will appear. As Socrates might have asked: Do we really need to let things rest at the present level of desperation?

SUMMARY OF PART THREE:

Part Three confirms what Part Two was already telling us: humans cannot know or connect with themselves or others or with reality. The ironic reason is that we are real already but we believe we are separate. This illusion is created when we adopt the vantage point of the self. The attempt to satisfy the demands of the self and the socio has produced a politicised society. Socrates makes it abundantly clear that this is an intellectual failure. He shows that we can only conceive of the human as the animation generated by the in-between. This is expressed in many terms – otherness, the interpersonal, conversation, friendship or Agora-spirit. Only when we are free of the self can we explore these possibilities. New questions now tumble out of old ones. The six approaches in this Part tell us what happens when we realise that reality is change and that we do not need to do anything about it. The problem is the self and the modern penchant for personal happiness. They have eclipsed the search for wholeness. The human potential revealed in this Part might indeed, as Socrates surmised, be capable of turning a passive citizenry into a liberated, animated one. He expected a liberated citizen to be capable of discerning the common root from which spring daily life and abstract thinking.

Philosophy too arises from the in-between. It shows the price we pay for clutching on to personhood, moral codes or social positions. The in-between says there is no need to adopt common values because the state of things is already disrupted by our entropic, chaotic dual-nature. Things cannot be possessed; assemblies fall apart; change is everywhere. So the in-between seeks to reveal the within as a gigantic cover-up. Logic, sense and rationality have corralled instincts and fears inside a person in order to maintain an external show of coping. Only when the in-between has done its job and revealed the within to be an act of bad faith can the in-between take us to monism. Only in this world of joined-up things will fear of each other and of ourselves evaporate.

Philosophy asks: Is there any way to handle consciousness that is not the cause of pain and death? We are back again in the city of Thebes overcome by calamity. The answer is again: the in-between. Socrates realised that this energy is released in the Agora. He was saying in effect that the problem lies in what we think of ourselves. It is actually fear of the infinite reach of consciousness. We deem ourselves incapable of handling infinity; meaninglessness by another name. This is Freud's 'death instinct,' which is anything that settles on an answer or a fixed position. It is what Freud calls a defence. But why is meaninglessness a problem? If we let life lead us we will defend ourself against a defence and thereby counter the death instinct. It must be remembered that life is indifferent, not antagonistic. We can't face life; rather, with all its bounty, it faces us. There is no need to panic.

Consciousness allows us to take a second look. Now the first look is diminished. We are no longer pinioned by it and can keep moving. We have stopped taking agency or control to the point where it runs out of control. Now no one is in control. Aporia, the Greek term for the state that Socrates' interlocutors fell into under his unremitting interrogation, means 'lacking absolute possibility of understanding.' The interlocutors were able to lose control. Only at this point can new ideas emerge and be processed and a true connection be made with others.

But a dispiriting thought arises. The in-between I have been lauding seems everywhere to be absent today; the within I feared becoming disproportionately large has turned out to be little more than a will o' the wisp. The joined-up world is but a chimera - selves move in splendid isolation sustained only by momentary bursts of imagination. Relationships and groups fall apart under the slightest challenge to self or identity. We have lost a sense of otherness and of the complexity of the human. Without them we cannot partake in harmony. So, are we doomed to face a brave new world in which, instead of venturing out to other people, humankind seeks 'reality' in social media, noisy disjunction, artistic timidity, and a machine-dominated form of life? We seem to have rejected the gift of logos and betrayed all that the Axial Age promised. Abandoning our personal positions and becoming inspired by others seem distant prospects.

This dystopian cul-de-sac can be avoided by remembering that humans are forever afraid of the effect they have on each other. Society and politics are based on the supposition that others might hurt me, and that it is the task of law to protect me. But philosophy encourages us to hypothesise that it is the opposite that truly obtains. Now we can consider the possibility that the human is driven by a fear of the harm he might do to others. It all comes back to the self. As a form of armour we build to protect ourselves against others it works well. But it keeps others out as well. We want protection but not protection's other side - a severance of love relations with others. 'Survivor's guilt' is a term used to describe a lingering sorrow for those we left behind as we ventured out into the world. We see ourselves as free only at their expense, and never make a clean break. We then baulk at the idea of making close relations with others. Otherness is a step too far until we address this inhibition.

A public lack of appreciation of the crucial role of the in-between or otherness need not throw us off our own beat. Philosophy is not a radical or outre version of what we presently know. Indeed, it doesn't seek to provide answers or to change things at all. It asks us instead to generate new, more challenging questions about everything we claim to know. It accepts the idea that change is built into the universe, that the universe is change. Accordingly, philosophy sets the spirit of curiosity, the love of wisdom, on a metaphysical journey. But first, this spirit must manifest itself at the individual level. It cannot be taught; it does not respond to cajolery or persuasion. Goodness, ethical probity and political compromise will be revealed as what happens when we have not dealt with our survivor's guilt. A spirit of curiosity about everything will have emerged, driven by a blind sense of urgency. The individual's technical prowess is a secondary matter here; practical or lived philosophy is not a bookish venture. Indeed, it is a second move. It doesn't anticipate trouble or provide a manual for resolving daily tribulations (even though it helps indirectly). The Axial breakthrough was the understanding that the human is an idea. When Axial thinkers ontologised ideas they did so with reference to the human, knowing that only by stepping beyond the discrete and personal can humans be addressed. They were responding to the question: What is a human? and not: What is a body or a rock? They accomplished what we have struggled with ever since. They understood that individuals are afraid when looking at the world from within, taking an 'I' position or trying to validate the inner life wholesale. And that by taking the position of an observer the human can re-cognise the world, find a place in it, and pre-empt anxiety or fear. The ancients didn't understand the socio. But we can see that it builds on self-contradictions. Ironically, by philosophising the self, we have rescued it, helped it find its place in reality and saved it from an anxiety-creating search for an internal grounding. It is now complete and fully realised.

CONCLUSION

It is little wonder that the Sphinx treated humanity as a riddle. We think metaphorically about everything and then respond to these metaphors, a move that keeps reality at arms' length. We live as if in the penumbra of a shadow cast by reality. Here we dance with metaphors until, so to speak, the moment that reality reins us in. The ability to think metaphorically means that there is no end to what humans can do. This is what makes the human a riddle. The question of the human cannot be answered: there is no fixed point to be reached. Questioning only provokes further explorations of the gap between consciousness and reality. We straddle a mind-body divide. But this has the effect of making us 'other' to ourselves. To expect a descriptive, logical, causal or consequential answer to the question is to miss the point: we have entered the realm of complexity where Heraclitus' 'unity of opposites' may be our clearest lead. This makes us half-gods and half-mortals, in other words, daemons.

Humans are what is left after the retreat from the Agora. For long moments we can hypothesise Socrates' interlocutors glimpsed truth as they braved encounters in that cauldron of interaction. Their minds were free of introspection and unburdened by a social mind-set. As a community of enquirers they occupied an idealised space even as they faced each other in a physical public square. The exercise was an invocation of pure process in those moments. Nothing stopped the flow, neither acts of will or narration, nor professions of feeling such as 'I love/hate you.' Nervous reactions to the indeterminacy of the flow were salved by a general trust in the efficacy of process. Since then, in the absence of a Socrates to chivvy people along, humanity has succumbed to the temptation to worship idols, to quest after the 'being' of humans, to cling to a romantic notion of family, and to slip into the self-determined mind-trap of society. This has unknowingly released floods of emotional acting-out. The idea of psychosis has been pushed to the margin of discourse. Neurosis has heedlessly been allowed to generate social action, and then to develop more neurosis out of this action. The human body we see in front of us (the embodied child, partner, friend, or adversary) has been made to carry all the expectations that only the idea of a human can carry.

The riddle of the Sphinx reminds us that we ignore reality at our cost. It tells us that the possibilities open to humans are too many to be contained in formulae or significations. Humans are not susceptible of being treated as an object of enquiry. They come forward as agents, presenting themselves as actors at the centre of things and not as objects to be studied. An attempt to tie them down amounts only to the building of a mental construction. Indeed, the high degree of human interrelatedness invalidates such a move. And even so their 'coming forward' is a half-hearted affair. Only when the human spirit is diminished by fear of close encounters do people seem to communicate, and then only in highly guarded, colloquial or formal ways. When people are free to converse uninhibitedly - and the Agora is just such an attempt - they fear each other too much and hold back. The Agora was a space where people could celebrate the energy of the in-between. It was assumed they could handle their fears and not invoke the law for protection. But things move fast in that space; participants are opened-up to the point that an opportunity to pin things down disappears completely, leaving only a vapour trail of the process of interaction.

Every move has failed but philosophy. It is a corrective move; it deconstructs unexamined language and thoughts. It is available to be applied to humanity just before it reaches the brink. It can do this because philosophy is not *a* method but *the* method. It tilts the mind away from a belief in the efficacy of experience, away from what one habitually thinks, feels or does, and turns humans into witnesses of the world. The Greeks looked at things from outside; moderns look at them as subjective insiders. Philosophy is a second move: it acknowledges what is happening and then questions it unrelentingly. When it takes thinking to the absolute level it is saying that agency lies in the universe and not in the person or in what we are looking at. Left alone, the self perpetually turns inwards. Here, thinking is stultified by victim-inducing feelings. The sum total of the world's misery is constantly enhanced. Thus our inability to handle the gift of consciousness has left us at the mercy of (what we take to be) our experiences and feelings. They turn us into wretched victims. But personal experience is too narrow to be a reliable guide to things in general. Rather, as nourishment for the ego, it is a cause of loneliness. When humans direct consciousness inwards they act as if this amounts to an engagement with the outside world. What they perceive is only a product of the mind's inner workings. But we are not the opposite of a pebble, that is, pure mind; we are a pebble plus. We struggle with this thought. Indeed the biggest problem for humans is that life in the world outside the self is so full.

Original sin starts outside, in life. For example, a friend does something that shocks me. I immediately become afraid of their otherness, of that which I cannot comprehend or anticipate. My state of shock prevents me questioning the framework into which my mind has placed the action. I forget that my friend and I have so much in common and, rather than letting things follow their course (and thereby trusting in reality), I define this occurrence as a problem, try to solve it, and immediately create others. The superego is forever seeking to balance (and if not balance then numb) the 'I.' It diverts us from life. The more we attempt to solve problems, the more the after-effects of earlier ones pile up; life seems to be a never-ending exercise in kicking the ball further down the road. People become their own worst enemies because they unquestioningly accept what the mind presents to them as reality. And yet every perception is mind-generated. Full of social imperatives, the mind interprets a simple occurrence as a threat to the ego. I feel 'I am angry.' But the mind won't stop niggling at the issue, which soon transforms into 'I am intrigued by anger.' It is as if anger is a charismatic friend before whom I must prostrate myself. So life goes on. And yet, as Spinoza reminds us, life can be full of joy! Where do we turn?

One place is consciousness: we think about it as a gift beyond compare. Indeed, when it is applied to an object or idea it can lift the lid on all that we take for granted. But it is also the deadliest adversary when it escapes philosophical scrutiny. Left unattended it becomes enamoured of itself. Excitation then breeds unchecked. Glamour, intensity, celebrity, narcissism: all emanate from the self-regard which consciousness produces. Excitement grows in the light cast by appearance. Animation is no longer found in the very process of relating but in the regard shown to the appearances that relationships throw off. But this is not all. The process that philosophy generates has its own dark side. We begin to understand now that we are not entities. We are too affected by others for that to obtain. The threat of oblivion looms. Consciousness has carried us beyond the concretion of things to a sense of totality we have never accessed hitherto. Yet we do not need to perceive the resulting 'chaos' as madness. Indeed it is utter sanity. When we shed the carapace of the self we can stop giving credence to our unexamined thoughts or feelings. We can now see them as configurations of thought we've adopted from others.

We can resolve every quandary by turning to others. But initially things can go awry because relationships have been thoroughly infiltrated by social values. Socrates advocated vigilance in the face of these threats. He urged us to become the audience in the world and not a player in a spectacle. The spectacle arises from narcissism. He suggested we observe our life rather than forever be embroiled in it. As an observer/audience we can understand the role and interaction of others on stage. The observer acts as witness of the world without accruing guilt for the mess created by the roles people fill. The key move is to avoid becoming enmeshed in these roles. We need not change ourselves but instead learn to use ourselves. We can for example realise that we do not 'feel' upset; instead, the feeling connects us to the idea of being upset. We can find relief only when we treat consciousness as a metaphor and place it outside ourselves.

The idea of a person is not sufficiently philosophised. Here is a major task for philosophy. The distress caused when we accept experiences as if they are our own is not inevitable. Psychology offers itself as an alternative here of course. But philosophy wins hands down. It offers understanding of distress in the broadest context without resort to techniques of intervention and it takes place in the public square, that is, where citizens interact intensely. Psychology in contrast argues from techniques and not understanding; it is an updated version of the confessional where one person's sins are acknowledged to another. Philosophy would argue that understanding is enough to release a person from distress; that there are no insane people, and that what is lacking is a preparedness to look into insanity. Psychology's limitations arise from an assumption that the patient is not there as a functioning self until the practitioner brings them into being. But it is a valid move to change this assumption and hypothesise that the patient is already there as much or more than the practitioner. The patient's socialising processes have already been breached whereas the practitioner's remain intact. In any case, the patient is just as capable of possessing a deep sense of self or enlightenment as the practitioner. When we reverse these assumptions, we can see that therapy does not touch any wellsprings. A strong case can be made that society would benefit from a diversion of some of the money spent on mental health to a profound investigation into human relating and sociability.

The human stands out from other species because its core is split. It can accept that the body will die, but it will doggedly resist the thought that the mind will stop functioning. As a result it is afraid of its own feelings and thoughts and of other human beings. It is defensive and at the same time it hunts things down. Its art and culture constrain differences between things to manageable levels. They are able to diagnose the diminishment they impose but cannot offer a radical way out. Culture and art lack the courage to tell us exactly how it is. They raise the spirits and then leave them dangling.

Accordingly humans find it extremely difficult to accept that their nature lies within the nature of all things. The irony is that, for humans to benefit from this insight, they would have to direct their consciousness outwards beyond the human. Socrates adds cosmology to the question of how to live a life. This is not to say that the issue resolves itself into a clash between cosmology and the human but that a reorientation is required. A first move would be to admit that cosmology has a part to play. Indeed Socrates and Plato refused to focus myopically on human psychology. Since then, Hellenistic schools such as Stoicism have turned attention back to the human again. The fascination of humans with themselves seems to know no bounds. And so the challenge for us is to place ourselves back in the cosmos, so to speak, or behind the camera rather than in front of it. This move allows us to discover things for their own sake. We will discover ourselves in the process. A thing is for-itself before enquiry. In humans it generally sinks down to become a thing-in-itself. Philosophical enquiry elevates the thing-in-itself until it is a thing-for-itself again, a radical move. We are now able to address the nature of things. The steps ascend from the lowest which puts a specific person ahead of us to the next, which puts anyone ahead. At the highest level we put otherness ahead.

Now the place of the in-between comes to the fore. It helps the thing-in-itself to reveal that we do not know who we are until we are connected to others. As we enquire into it, the other unravels and relates back. What has become clear is that the in-between is the nature of the other. Otherwise we would relate only to its appearance. When we relate to the other we enter into their core, but only at the meta or conceptual level of the in-between. At this level there is no 'I' or 'other.' They have given way to the concept of the in-between. We have reached the metaphysical point where we appreciate there are only concepts. This could never be achieved outside relationships: appearance would merely meet appearance. Philosophical enquiry is an active fascination that enables us to understand that which is the 'mystery' of the other. I stress the word 'that' because it is always already, given, primordial, a priori. In other words, it lies in the zone of expanded reality known as is-ness.

Put another way, our journey to the other is away from the construction of thoughts to the processing of thought without limit. This move prevents perceptions imposing rigidities on the indeterminacy of reality. We must disturb old thoughts (aporia) before we can rid ourselves of the burden of self. Only then are we able to love what we hitherto judged to be disgusting or ugly. We can then feel good or real in the world because we have owned up to our fears. We can return all particulars to the absolute once we admit that our wanting to be naughty and disturb the conformity of the ruck arises from joie de vivre and not from moral turpitude.

The Platonic tradition sets up thoughts, impressions or feelings as opposites of each other as an opening gambit. Plato describes Socrates' efforts to establish which component was the lesser and which the larger, and then to collapse the former into the latter. This move reveals more of each notion, thereby helping us to see how they relate together. It can become clear for example that one notion is a subset, part or aspect of the other. For example, anti-social behaviour can be seen as an aspect of ignorance. Anti-social behaviour implies a specific action or set of actions, whereas ignorance denotes the absence of specificity. The key distinction I am making is between the human and the world. I collapse the former into the latter. Of course I must remove my own humanity and self at the outset so that I do not become embroiled in the exercise.

Likewise, we must 'collapse' the human into the world in full recognition that it is already there anyway. To think otherwise is to deny the ubiquity of reality. This is the great human fallacy. Actual humans easily become feckless and romantic; they are drawn hither and thither by sparkling baubles and romantic dreams. They are both inside and outside reality at the same time. We expect a particular boy- or girl-friend, coat, car, job, or holiday destination to resolve all our human dilemmas. This is fantasy, un-reality. The answer to this Janus-faced, in-out relation to reality is to put everything into reality. Even the self can be reborn out of reality: I am the self who is moulded by the forces of reality, not by a wish to fit into society. I fearlessly hear what everyone says, full-force and unedited, and let it go to my core. I can now, and only now, say the other creates me. Open and fearlessly frank relationships are the cauldron out of which emerges this new version of self. The other gives me an opportunity I can't give myself. Humans cannot perceive themselves as 'I am'; they are too complex and changeable. To be a particular self or identity is a choice; it remains a figment of the mind. But we do not need to choose between self and reality in the other person; they are both an identity and real at the same time. This gives us an invaluable opportunity to ignore what they want us to hear, and instead listen intently to what is behind their words. Now we can hear who they are, their soul or essence. In philosophical terminology we see, not what they are or how they seek to present themselves, but that they are.

As we register this, we start to understand that perception cries out for attention. Perhaps inevitably biases and prejudices contained in crystallised experiences colour incoming reality. The problem here is consciousness. It goes hunting for reality and as it does so its gaze settles on an object which it then seeks to possess. Behind this move lies the dynamic of the subject-object relationship. Consciousness operates through a subject which falls in love with the object it desires. But objects are real and subjects are ossified versions of soul or reality. It is the object and not the subject that possesses agency in Greek philosophy. In other words, the universe reaches out to us, not us to it. The Greeks claimed that the object will lead us back to reality. This is why philosophy seeks to free objects from the gaze of subjects. A quick answer to this problem is to relax and do less and to let perception become less intense. The less we do the less the subject will lock onto the object.

But a longer-term resolution demands that we give attention to the mind. Ultimately it is the mind that grasps onto objects. It is not for nothing that in Greek myth Tiresias the seer was blind. In a sense we must blind ourselves to perception. The need for this drastic step arises because, when we tell ourselves we perceive the other, we are in fact picking up their perceptions. To make matters worse, their perceptions contain the 'me' who is perceiving them. This is a hall of mirrors. Our task is to convert these appearances into reality. The first step is to admit one's ignorance of reality in the face of these complexities. Now philosophical method enters: it takes us away from human suppositions that make us jump to conclusions and instead opens up an unmediated connection to the object or other. Our ignorance can initially be reduced by asking other people: what do you think is happening? They have their perceptions too of course. But, social conformity aside, we will gain the benefit of a more varied set of vantage points that might help to correct our own. However, an even more revealing move is to switch our attention from what we see to what we hear. The story of the blind seer is pertinent again. The eye quickly judges and contextualises things in terms of their beauty. The eye makes a strong claim to veracity. People exclaim: 'I saw it' and believe that such a claim clinches an argument. The ear is more passive and allows more reality to enter before it reacts. We are more likely to ask: 'What did I actually see?' than 'What did I actually hear?'

Plato anticipated these moves. He points to love as an impulse towards the other that carries us to the reality that lies beyond the appearance of both of us. He suggests two moves: suspend what we see; and then let love as an enquiry carry us back into the real world. The journey requires that we question our perceptions of the world until at last we move from a realm that is a product of our inner self to one anchored in the world outside.

Even so, the space between other people and me will not suddenly open to new thoughts simply because we have stopped filling it with socially-inflected opinions and judgements. A new form of conversation is called for, and we must actively participate in this development. Previously we offered the other person what we thought of as a bag of jewels - the fixed positions or opinions we have established during our lifetime, and they replied in kind. But now we can stay open to all that the other conveys, to the deepest messages they offer behind the spoken words. The intentness of our listening makes the other feel heard. With growing confidence they draw on long-hidden yearnings, disappointments and dreams. Leibowitz claims the other only emerges when we suspend our sense of self. We do not need to think what to say; the content of the conversation is not the issue.

And of course there is now no 'I' that thinks. Instead it is thought that thinks. Conversation is now transformative: it changes as it develops and it draws the parties into unexpected juxtapositions. Nothing has come from something; conversation leaves the old frames of reference behind on a journey to infinity. Thoughts follow a certain line and then suddenly make a detour to draw in something mentioned earlier, before stepping ahead of the general drift in anticipation of a thought that is only half-realised, and so on. The rescue or interjection of an old thought can change the present direction. Some thoughts are left on the shelf to be drawn on later, although they might be sacrificed to the prevailing flow.

We have returned to the central question of otherness. By another name, it is animation, consciousness or an irrepressible stirring. It is the totality of humans, God, an all-pervasive idea; it is psychosis. But above all it is what the thinkers of the Axial Age were working their way towards, driven by an immense dissatisfaction with the injunction to 'know thyself.' This injunction opens up a bottomless pit in which tormented souls search inside themselves for that which moves the universe. It must be remembered that Socrates was condemned because he destroyed the illusion that people are individuals and are somehow signally different from each other. Unfortunately Freud played into this view by asking his clients to find an inner space where all about them would be revealed.

But Socrates was pointing out that inner and outer spaces are the same thing, that the soul and the universe resonate as one. And, most crucially, that neither is located in the self. Plato told us that what most moves any one of us moves us all. There is no individuality: we move alike. Animation and imagination move in all directions at once; all manifestations boil down to group process. When we feel and do not defend against it we can be said to be experiencing ontology. The specialness of humans simply amounts to a participation in the spirit of the universe.

I have depicted is-ness as an expanded reality. Until we are clear what is omitted from reality we must make do with it for now as the only concept that pertains to all things. Plato told us that a concept taps into the potential that lies hidden behind a mental or social construct, a bout of emotionality or a physical entity. He also told us that, until humans bring thought to bear on otherness, an engagement is not real. In everyday terms this means that a conversation must deal with the relation between the conversationalists (and not merely focus on third-party issues like politics, football or the weather). Otherwise, both of them will remain a simulacrum of reality.

The idea of God serves us well at this juncture. Building on Leibowitz's ideas we can say a human is that which orients itself towards the idea of God. A human lies outside reality while orienting itself towards reality. Moreover, when will replaced nature in the Garden of Eden, all restrictions on human development were removed. There is now no anchor in nature, and no need for one. Transcendent Will connects us to a non-existent God, to an idea of God. Thus, although we cannot know God, we can stand before the Idea. Indeed we are condemned a la existentialism to stand before Him (or life in the case of existentialism) and commit to all the choices we make. Human relationship is only possible because of this move for, without the God of the philosophers, humans are too excitable and too porous to others' feelings to be able to engage with Transcendent Will. Moreover, standing before God involves more than just facing into a space beyond reality. It means that humans who stand there are an idea too. It means that every human who stands in this space is at least part-god or daemon.

The Axial Age did something amazing, probably something unique. It told us to step out of what we know as life and become an observer of it. Then we will stop fearing that we will disappear into the other as we come closer to them. Reality is now whatever is not me. Now and only now can I get to know it. Knowing is not connecting; it is something less than this. It means that as I engage with the other I am able to continue thinking about them and the world. Being able to think means not only that I will avoid fusing with them, i.e. not succumb to erotic love. It also follows I will not rebound from this fusing. In other words, the possibility of a fruitful long-term relationship arises. To be sure, I will never know reality fully, but I will gain knowledge of it. This resolves issues thrown up by the human condition, which arise from being in nature and being conscious of it at the same time. It may seem something of a let-down – no direct, one-to-one connection! - but what a cornucopia of wonders it opens up.

Philosophy is the holder of the human. In effect it says to humankind: 'You are foregone and corrupted. But I know what you are capable of.' Philosophy helps things fall into place. It is the bearer of truth, the Solomonic mother who gave up her child rather than risk its death. It doesn't set out to save people by winning an argument, coming to a conclusion, or leaping into action. Like Oedipus, it recognises that we may win the glittering prize and become king but, in so doing, will risk losing our core or soul as we engage with people wholly on terms laid down by society. We must then, like Oedipus again, bow before fate and seek redemption through suffering.

But that is the message of mythos. In that age an heroic warrior aristocracy sought to infuse meaning into their lives by seeking a 'good' death. But Sophocles' play rises above this kind of metaphor: he uses the age-old riddle of the Sphinx simply for ironic effect. Behind the heightened emotions of the story of Oedipus he leaves space for logos to emerge. He is a philosopher in spirit. He is saying that the riddle of the human that is voiced by the Sphinx is a myth, a story, in the same way that the Sphinx is a fiction and the play itself a fiction. He performs a triple-entendre, a supreme example of Socratic irony. Sophocles' great insight is that there is not even a riddle waiting to be unravelled. It is all smoke and mirrors. Greek drama, like its philosophy, was not meant to provide answers but to see beyond the confines of our narrow selfhood. We've been blinded by the narrative of humanity, by our sense of specialness. There is no problem to be solved. Consciousness never did remove us from reality. We are real already and it was ever thus.

ENDNOTES
Introduction

1)   Roberto Calasso, *The Marriage of Cadmus and Harmony* (New York, Alfred A. Knopf, 1993) p 344.

Chapter One: Expulsion from Nature.

1)   *Stanford Encyclopedia of Philosophy*. See also: 'A true recognition of God is only the recognition that no man can recognise God.' Yeshayahu Leibowitz, *Accepting the Yoke of Heaven*: *Commentary on the Weekly Torah Portion* (Jerusalem, Urim Publications, 2006 edition) p 60.

Chapter Two: The Starting Point: The Axial Age.

1)   These four moves allow humans to escape the self. What is generally meant by love today is what the Greeks called Eros. This is an intense conjoining, a fusing of two selves.   Rather, I mean philia and particularly agape; both are more accepting of difference and otherness. The muse is an idea in Greek myths that inspires us; literally, it breathes into us air from the universe that we have been lacking. The in-between was mentioned in the Note on Methodology. It is energy generated in the company of others that allows us to transcend actuality and encounter 'otherness,' radical non-me-ness. The meta is a concept of thinking that bridges dichotomies and thereby clears our path to the absolute. Taken together, these four moves free humans to return to the flux of reality and counter the ossifying

proclivity of the self. All have the power to release thought or consciousness into the world and reveal the connection between all things.

Chapter Four: The Human as a Being.

1)   Joseph Agassi, *A Philosopher's Apprentice: In Karl Popper's Workshop*; Revised, Extended and Annotated Edition (Amsterdam and New York, Rodopi, 2008) p 297.

Chapter Five: The Human and the Expression of Feelings.

1)   Lisa Feldman Barrett, *How Emotions are Made: The Secret Life of the Brain* (London, Pan Books, 2018).

2)   Stephen R C Hicks, *Explaining Postmodernism: Skepticism and Socialism from Rousseau to Foucault.* Expanded Edition (Redland Bay, Queensland, Connor Court Publishing, 2019) pp 81, 82.

Chapter Six: The Human and the Family.

1)   Gilles Deleuze and Felix Guattari, *Anti-Oedipus: Capitalism and Schizophrenia* (London, Continuum, 2004) p 52.

2)   CS Lewis, *The Four Loves* (London, HarperCollins, 2002 edition) p 52.

3)   Friedrich Engels, *The Origins of the Family, Private Property and the State* (1884; Harmondsworth, Penguin,1985 edition) p 35.

4)   Jose Luis Moreno Pestana, 'Jacques Donzelot's The Policing of Families (1977) in Context,' in Robbie Duschinsky and Leon Antonio Rocha (eds) *Foucault, the Family and Politics* (Basingstoke, Palgrave MacMillan, 2012) p 133.

5)   Alain Badiou, *In Praise of Love* (London, Serpent's Tail, 2012) pp 49-50.

6)   Deleuze and Guattari, *Ibid.*, p 97.

Chapter Seven: The Human and Society.

1)   Most strongly associated with the writings of Stanley Fish. Quoted in Hicks, *Ibid.*, pp 234-235.

Chapter Eight: The Human and the Socio.

1)   Thucydides, *The Peloponnesian War* (Book Two, Chapter 40).

2)   Gilles Deleuze and Felix Guattari, *What is Philosophy?*   (New York, Columbia University Press, 1994) pp 126-1

Chapter Twelve: The Human emerges from Speech.

1)   Gilbert Murray, *Hellenism and the Modern World* (London, George Allen and Unwin, 1953) p 27.

2)   Maurice Blanchot, *The Infinite Conversation* (Minneapolis, University of Minnesota Press, 1993) p 28.

Chapter Thirteen: The Human emerges in Friendship.

1)   Badiou, *Ibid.*, p 26.

2)   Lewis, *Ibid.*, pp 70-71.

3)   David Smail, *Taking Care: An Alternative to Therapy* (1987; London, Karnac, 2015).

Chapter Fourteen: The Human emerges in the Agora.

1)   Murray, *Ibid.*, p 35.

2)   Frisbee Sheffield, 'Socrates and the Ethics of Conversation,'   https://antigonejournal.com/2021/04/Socrates-ethics-conversation/

3)   Bettany Hughes, *The Hemlock Cup: Socrates, Athens, and the Search for the Good Life* (Alfred A Knopf, 2011) p 22.

4)   CS Lewis, *The Problem of Pain* (1940; London, HarperCollins, 2002 edition) p 158.

BIOGRAPHICAL NOTE

Roy Sturgess taught economic history in universities in England, Scotland and the United States and was a research associate in Palestine. He is a member of the Saturday group where issues that emerge from society or from interactions in the group are conceptualised in the spirit of Socrates' humanisation of natural philosophy.

INDEX

www.ingramcontent.com/pod-product-compliance
Lightning Source LLC
Chambersburg PA
CBHW071412090426
42737CB00011B/1439